AGING
AND THE
HUMAN CONDITION

AGING AND THE
HUMAN CONDITION

Edited by

Gari Lesnoff-Caravaglia, Ph.D.

Sangamon State University
Springfield, Illinois

Volume II, Frontiers in Aging Series
Series Editor: Gari Lesnoff-Caravaglia, Ph.D.

HUMAN SCIENCES PRESS, INC.
72 FIFTH AVENUE,
NEW YORK, N.Y. 10011

Printed in the United States of America
23456789 987654321

Library of Congress Cataloging in Publication Data

Main entry under title:

Aging and the human condition.

    (Frontiers in aging series; v. 2)
    Includes index.
    1. Aging—Addresses, essays, lectures. 2. Death—Psychological aspects—Addresses, essays, lectures. I. Lesnoff-Caravaglia, Gari. II. Series.
HQ1061.A4573   305.2′6   LC 81–6630
ISBN 0–89885–029-0   AACR2

CONTENTS

CONTRIBUTORS

Clifford Alexander, Ph.D., Coordinator Gerontology Program, Department of Social Welfare, University of Nevada, Las Vegas, Nevada

Robert C. Atchley, Ph.D., Director, Scripps Foundation Gerontology Center, Miami University, Oxford, Ohio

Dorothy Demby, A.C.S.W., National Specialist on Aging, American Foundation for the Blind, New York, New York

Ira F. Ehrlich, D.S.W., Professor/Division, Social and Community Services, Southern Illinois University, Carbondale, Illinois

Phyllis Ehrlich, M.S.S.A., Assistant Professor, Rehabilitation Institute, Southern Illinois University, Carbondale, Illinois

Antony G. N. Flew, D. Litt., Professor of Philosophy, University of Reading, Reading, England

Robert Fulton, Ph.D., Professor/Director, Center for Death Education and Research, University of Minnesota, Minneapolis, Minnesota

David O. Moberg, Ph.D., Professor, Department of Sociology, Anthropology, and Social Work, Marquette University, Milwaukee, Wisconsin

Daniel G. O'Hare, S. J., Jesuit Community, Washington, D.C.

Irving Rosow, Ph.D., Professor, Langley Porter Institute, University of California, San Francisco, California

E. Percil Stanford, Ph.D., Director, University Center on Aging, San Diego State University, San Diego, California

Gordon F. Streib, Ph.D., Graduate Research Professor, Department of Sociology, University of Florida, Gainesville, Florida

INTRODUCTION

One of the significant features of the human condition is the structure of time, for time provides the framework within which we perceive and exercise human possibilities. Time, however, is generally considered from a limited perspective and is viewed in a segmented fashion; it is parceled out according to periods of work, play, rest, and meals. More extensive planning is devoted to long-range time segments involving career goals, school attendance, marriage, and special opportunities such as vacations or holidays. Holidays serve as peak points in time, as much behavior is influenced by holiday expectations.

Exceptions to such time perception can be found among young children and the old. As experienced by the young, time is almost without boundaries and appears as a continuous flow. The end of life, death, is rarely taken into consideration. The decrease in infant mortality, along with medical advances that make death for young persons in our culture a remote possibility, allow the younger person to adopt a view of time that borders on the limitless. Such a view, however, hampers the perception of life as a cumulative developmental process.

Older persons, on the other hand, do not plan as if time were unlimited. Since they realize that the close of life is at hand, limits are set to desires, expectations, and hopes. Such life experience is sharpened by the appreciation that events, once past, are really beyond recall. Awareness of the future, and the knowledge of one's own personal future which derives from this, is based on the expectation that time will bring something new in its wake. A willingness to face certain coming events forms an important part of the temporal structure which establishes the perimeter of people's lives. If this awareness of the future is lost, the structure breaks down and all that remains to provide form or an anchor to life is the routine of daily survival.

For older persons, time is utilized and perceived in a very restricted fashion. Days may be viewed from the perspective of personal needs. Events such as rising in the morning, preparing breakfast, and tidying up become moments of some significance. This is particularly true when the individual is advanced in age, or when physical movement is limited, and the successful accomplishment of even small tasks requires much personal attention and effort.

Such restrictions to a continuous present force the older individuals to focus on whatever physical debilities and ailments they may have. Greater attention is directed to the physical self, and such lives are lived in a present that is devoid of content. Life in a continuous present that is unrelieved by interaction with the past or by expectation of hope in the future is exposed to the menace of unspeakable boredom.

Such boredom is a living death—an antechamber for the biological event. The modern age is much more death-oriented than we have been led to believe. The empty days of old age are still waters of experience similar to the "nonlived life" brought on by drug abuse.

The full realization that life must come to an end places the older individual in a situation which cannot be changed and from which there is no escape. Nonetheless, some older persons attempt to develop personal possibilities that in some sense have a posthumous goal. When older people decide to learn a foreign language, they are not always exclusively prompted by a desire for new knowledge. Often the foreign language serves as a goal they know they will never reach. Plans of unlimited duration, whose realization is set at a point in the very distant future, are said to prolong life. This may also account for the great interest that older persons manifest in gardening, for a garden provides endless work.

Human existence, in its most simplest terms, is a condition that may be, or may not be. This quality colors the possibilities to which individuals may aspire. For example, everything that an individual may hope to become, want to learn, or dream to achieve—all these are nothing more than possibilities. To give reality to any of these possibilities, an individual must choose. When people choose, they expect that they have an array of choices. The number and variety of these choices will vary with situations, the individual, the social climate in which the person lives, and the operative social expectations. All of these factors will have a bearing on the number of choices open to an individual, as will the individual's awareness that the possibilities exist. It may well be that there are possibilities within given situations which the individual will not perceive because of self-perceptions, societal norms, or cultural expectations.

Liberation movements often direct their efforts toward extending the entire range of choices. The women's liberation movement of the late 1960s and 70s is a case in point. Struggles for equal rights have as their basis the enlarging of the horizon for individual choice. In a very real sense, possibility lies at the heart of human freedom.

Such concern with human possibilities, however they may be limited by age, illness, and a variety of disabilities, is no longer a purely academic question. The women's liberation movement is rapidly tearing down the barrier that sex presented, in much the same way that blacks have largely inserted themselves as participating members of American society. The search for identity and recognition on the part of minority groups such as Jews, Poles, and Mexican-Americans, has further contributed to a broader perception of the problems of human beings, along with an increased sensitivity to particular group concerns. These movements are, at bottom, an expression of a growing concern of large segments of the population for a realistic appraisal of their possibilities in the world.

Older persons have yet to make such a dramatic appeal.

Their lack of ability to present such a united effort is partly due to their failure to see themselves as a separate and distinct entity within society; they relate more easily to their particular social or ethnic group rather than to the age group. Subgroups within the older population, such as the elderly single room occupant, add to the difficulties of such single definition.

This lack of perception of themselves as a group is also hampered by society's denial of the aging process, and negative stereotyping which makes it demeaning and embarrassing to admit to one's true age. Such denial, like the denial of any natural event or process in society, leads to aberrations. As a result we have panic associated with menopause, panic and little preparation for retirement, and real fear of the process of aging itself, which has unfortunately been painted as a series of losses with few gains to be anticipated.

Even though the individual may feel free to choose the direction of his or her life, including how to deal with the limitations of old age, there is still one more overriding restriction, a restriction that older individuals are probably more aware of than any other age group. The one element that coexists with all possibility is the possibility of death. Death can effectively eliminate all possibilities, including the individual to whom they belong. (For possibilities do *belong* in the sense that *my* possibilities are mine, and another individual's are *his* or *hers*, even when shared. In marriage, for example, each individual still approaches this situation in a unique fashion.) It is extremely difficult to face the possibility of death when society so effectively manages to cloak it from view and exclude it from human possibility.

Such limitations imposed on persons are complex features of societies and cultures, and they create a web between personal experience and aspiration, and societal expectations and norms. Where individual action begins and ends is as difficult to determine as is the thread of cultural and societal influence. Yet within such intertwining, human beings seek out areas of individual determination in which to impress their uniqueness or some sense of *I* upon the fleeting moments of human experience.

It has been said that the American nation has never really experienced tragedy, and that Americans have never really known its meaning. This, in part, has contributed to the national

American optimism. Nonetheless, millions of Americans are beginning to know tragedy through experiences such as growing old and dying in old age. For many older persons, sheer survival has become a deliberate daily project.

This is the real significance of the word *tragedy*—not simply defeat and grief, but the pain of having to struggle to establish and certify one's significance in the world. In this sense, the older American has begun to develop, in the philosopher Unamuno's phrase, the tragic sense of life.

Gari Lesnoff-Caravaglia
Sangamon State University
Springfield, Illinois

Chapter 1

ELDERLY IN TRANSITION

E. Percil Stanford and Clifford Alexander

By now it is no secret that the elderly of the world are more than a temporary social force to be recognized. The elderly are becoming more significant in determining the texture of societies throughout the world. The mere strength and ability of societies to survive now and in the future will increasingly depend on our ability to find a meaningful place for the older people of the world. We should keep in mind some of the lessons learned from Leo Simmons's work, which was first published in 1945 (Simmons, 1945). He makes it clear that older people are an important part of the social fabric of most societies. We cannot afford to close the older people out of many facets of life which, were it not for them, we could not know or enjoy.

The 22 million or more persons who are 65 and over in this country alone serve as an indication of the magnitude of the resource older people represent. It is reasonable to charge each citizen of this country with the responsibility of fully involving, as a matter of course, older adults in all aspects of life. It should not be a matter of always giving special attention to older citizens. Without doubt, it would be more to their liking to be given equal consideration in all facets of life without special policies, laws, and regulations.

Social awareness brought about by a few social activities has called attention to the uncertainty in the plight of the current and future elderly population in this country. During the last half of the 1970s, older people have become more dedicated advocates in their own behalf. The older advocate is a much more sophisticated person than historically perceived. Several organizations developed to carry the advocacy flag have leadership of a high caliber. The training and education, as well as the work experience of many leaders in these organizations, are the best this country can offer. At the same time, there are persons who have not had the education or work experience but are nonetheless thrown into the breach to chart new courses for themselves and their peers.

ADVOCACY

The assumption that older people want to be advocates in their own behalf has set the stage for some of our most significant legislation. For example, the Older Americans Act of 1965 developed partially around the idea that older people and those working in their behalf will be active advocates for their causes. The basic idea is sound, but the premise is weakened when the assumption broadens to consider that all older people want to be self-advocates. A large segment of the older population was never involved in political or social movements.

The active involvement of all older people in shaping their destiny is an honorable goal, but there is a missing ingredient: many nonwhite minority elders have for years been discouraged from involvement in shaping their social or political future. Many cases of physical abuse and even death can be cited as a result of attempts by blacks to make their will felt in the decision-making process (Stanford, 1975). Black people have been trying to become influential in politics for nearly a century and a half. It is significant that the struggle for the right to become involved has met with negative consequences, but has not been a complete failure. The forces to combat legitimate participation met with greater psychological success than most care to recognize. Older blacks are ever mindful that physical and emotional abuse has been a reality for them and many of their loved ones whenever they attempted to express an interest in determining their destiny by being involved in community affairs. We must keep the historical perspective in mind if we are to understand current circumstances and actions or nonactions. Critics of older blacks readily point out that older black persons (OBP) are not visible in meaningful ways, even though there are government laws and regulations specifying the inclusion of older minorities in general. The critics tend to dismiss quickly the history of forced nonparticipation. The masses of older blacks have not forgotten or forgiven their suppressors. A few years cannot erase the deep physical and emotional pain suffered when there was hope of active involvement. On occasion, black elderly will be open about why limited or no participation is a common pattern. Very few believe it will make any difference, and too many remember when their voice was not heard or, if heard, not recognized. "Why bother" has often become their byword.

Several factors appropriately figure into the matrix that explains the noninvolvement of many black elderly. An important ingredient appears to be formal education; many do not feel that they have the ability to match wits with their Anglo cohorts who may be involved at an equivalent level. Another more basic factor that is often not expressed is the fear of being embarrassed because of speech patterns, simple matters of protocol, or even what they wear. But seldom will anyone admit this. Instead they usually say that they have nothing to contribute or no transportation, that they are too busy, or that nothing they say will make a difference. In any event the end result is that the level of black elderly involvement continues to be too low.

It is not appropriate to end this statement on a flat or negative note. There has been considerable positive movement on the national level to ensure a greater impact on policy and program development by the black elderly themselves. For approximately eight years, the National Caucus on the Black Aged, for example, has taken leadership throughout the country to establish a mechanism for black elderly to have a say in determining how their social, political, and economic lives will be governed. Other mechanisms are beginning to surface. For example, many elderly blacks are now associated with a variety of professional or political organizations active in social and political causes. Their advice and counsel is often sought. Still, even though advice may be sought, it is often not used in the most strategic manner, if it is used at all.

BENEFIT PROGRAMS

Minority elders are frequently faced with the frustrating problem that the benefit programs available do not fully meet their needs. A complex system of agencies and programs attempts to serve older people in a variety of ways. But the public policy-making process, which makes several programs possible, does not look at the comprehensive way in which programs can be designed. Many programs created by legislative action are aimed at solving only one or a few problems of older individuals (Latham, 1965).

The major programs serving the elderly can be categorized into three major groupings: (1) programs in which age alone is the primary determinant of eligibility; (2) programs that use age and income as primary determinants of eligibility; and (3) programs that determine eligibility primarily by income and level of functioning; for example, some programs require that a recipient have a low income and some disability. A primary concern here is that the claims of the aged have been recognized through their inclusion in many of our federal policies and programs deliberately developed to meet the express needs of the aged. We have concluded that the aged do not constitute a homogeneous group, and that subgroups of older people have interests, attitudes, and other attributes that are shared by other members of society. Some programs, however, do have provisions for different approaches to different racially or ethnically defined subgroups of older people.

Whether intentionally or not, agencies and programs are often developed in fragmented and uncoordinated ways that lead to difficulties in providing meaningful services to many minority elders. The fact that most services are not geared to serving groups with cultural differences, including differences of language and perceptions of norm-responding day-to-day activities, can lead to insurmountable difficulties.

When looking at federal policies and programs, which seriously affect the minority older person, two issues emerge immediately. One is that there is very little research that examines the impact of public policies and programs on the minority older person. For that reason it becomes difficult to identify the specific administrative policies and mechanisms that create difficulties for the older individuals concerned. The best possible approach is for the basic input for administrative and legislative actions to flow from the people to the policy makers. Although many persons have voiced an understanding for this type of need, few in reality ever begin to practice what they espouse. One would have to agree with many activist older persons who say they have to know more about the real intent of some of the regulations and administrative mandates that drastically affect their lives. If they not only know more about the intent, but have a reasonable understanding of how some of the administrative-legislative decisions have been made, they can then perhaps better understand how to implement, interpret, and perhaps change some of those regulations that do not meet their needs.

The second issue, which derives from the first, is that no matter what the policy statements say or intend, the real benefits of those policies will not be felt unless they are in concert with the attitudes and values of the intended users. In recent months, it has been clear that although the Older Americans Act is intended to have a positive impact on minority groups, it is often misconstrued because of poor understanding of the values of some minority groups that want to take advantage of the legislation. This is not to say that each minority group should necessarily have specific legislation spelled out in the Older Americans Act.

Much has been said about the melting pot concept. It is a concept that has been meaningful for disparate sociological purposes, but it has had very adverse effects on many minority people, primarily because of the notion that there is more homogeneity among them than there really is. Categorically, it may be true that everyone must have certain basic needs met on a daily basis, but the great variation between such needs becomes apparent when the means by which those needs are met are examined closely. It is crucial to move more systematically toward accepting the fact that there is more actual diversity among minority groups than meets the eye. The subtleties in meeting cultural expectations are not always obvious. It is, however, the subtleties that render many well-intended programs and services ineffective.

A DEMOGRAPHIC VIEW

The black elderly population has been described in various terms by sociologists, economists, political scientists, social workers, and others. One of the first works in gerontology to have an impact on the intellectual community's attitude toward black older persons was *Double Jeopardy* (National Urban League, 1964; Lindsay, 1971). The overwhelming consensus of most gerontologists who are concerned with the black aged is, without qualification, that the social and economic plight of the black aged has improved very little during this decade. There is a great desire to determine how much some of the gaps have been widened or narrowed in several areas. But the major question continues to be whether there has been any change in a positive direction.

The black elderly population increases more than twice as fast as the overall black population. The total black population increased by 11% from 1970 to 1977, while the number of blacks 65 and over increased by 25% (from 1.6 million to 1.9 million), moving the portion of elderly persons in the total black population from 7 to 8% (U.S. Bureau of the Census, 1978a).

It is considerably interesting that there has been a change in the elderly population from rural to metropolitan areas. Indications are that between 1970 and 1977 the percentage of all blacks 65 and older who lived in metropolitan areas rose from 58 to 66%, while at the same time the percentage of elderly whites who lived in metropolitan areas climbed from 61 to 62%. More than half of the black aged in 1977 (55%) lived in central cities of the metropolitan areas, compared to only 29% of all the white elderly. At the beginning of the 1970s, a somewhat higher proportion of the white aged (32%) lived in central cities, compared to less than half (47%) of the black aged. It has become obvious that white older people are moving to the suburbs, while the black elders are continuing to move into the central cities. It is also apparent that at least one-third of all whites 65 and over now live in suburban areas, compared to possibly 11% of all black elderly (U.S. Bureau of the Census, 1978b).

LIFE EXPECTANCY

Many demographers have acknowledged that the life expectancy gap between blacks and whites has narrowed somewhat. In 1970 white men were expected to live 68.0 years, while black men were expected to live only 61.3 years—a gap of 6.7 years. But by 1976, white men had a life expectancy of 69.6 years, compared to a life expectancy at birth of 64.1 years among black men—a gap of 5.6 years (U.S. Public Health Service, 1978). The life expectancy gap between black and white women closed in a similar way. In 1970 white women could expect to live 75.6 years, while black women could expect to live only 69.4 years. However, by 1976 white women were expected to live 77.3 years, compared to 72.6 years for black women.

Among those who reach the age of 65, the life expectancies of both blacks and whites have been very close for some time. And even this small gap continues to close. From 1969 to 1971, the life expectancy of white men at age 65 was only slightly more (13.0 years) than the life expectancy of elderly black men (12.8). By 1976 the life expectancies of elderly black and white men were even closer (13.7 years for whites and 13.8 years for blacks). The trend for women is not significantly different. For example, while the life expectancy of white women at age 65 in 1969–1971 was a full year higher than the life expectancy for elderly black women (16.9 versus 15.9 years), this gap was cut in half by 1976 (18.1 versus 17.6 years).

INCOME

The amount of income, or lack of income, has been a practical as well as an intellectual issue for black elderly. There are some who like to point out that the income of elderly blacks has significantly improved during the 1970s. Between 1969 and 1976 the median income of elderly husband-wife black families increased 105% ($3,154 to $6,457), while the median income of elderly white husband-wife families increased 84% (from $4,827 to $8,902). These statistics show that the ratio of black to white income among husband-wife elderly families rose from 65 to 73% over those seven years (U.S. Bureau of the Census, 1978c).

One can see a more significant narrowing of the income gap in black and white families headed by elderly women. While the median income of elderly families headed by white women increased 66% between 1969 and 1976, the median income of elderly families headed by black women rose 91%. Therefore the black to white income ratio among families headed by women jumped from 44 to 51%.

The improvement in the income of elderly blacks extended to those who were living alone, as well as those who were living in families. The median income of black men living alone increased 120% (from $1,321 to $2,900) between 1969 and 1976, compared to an increase of 82% (from $2,336 to $4,245) among white men. For elderly women living alone, the increase in income over a seven-year period was about the same for blacks (102% from $1,263 to $2,547) and whites (90% from $1,838 to $3,497). Therefore, while the income ratio between elderly black and white women living alone remained essentially unchanged at about 70%, the black to white income ratio among elderly men rose from 67 to 68%.

The basic reason for the disproportionate improvement in the income status of the black elderly is that their incomes were so unreasonably low in 1969. Despite progress, the income of families headed by elderly black women continues to be only half that of the average family headed by an elderly white woman. Whether they are living in husband-wife families or alone, the incomes of elderly black men and women are only two-thirds that of their white counterparts. It is difficult to accept that the median income of elderly black families is significantly below the lowest level defined by the government as providing a minimum standard of living. In 1976 the Bureau of Labor Statistics' lower budget standard for a retired couple was $4,695. Approximately 17% of elderly white couples had incomes below that level, compared to 37% of elderly black couples. Thus poverty continues to characterize elderly blacks disproportionately more than whites.

The social and economic status of elderly blacks today is thought to be significantly better than it was 10 years ago. Between 1970 and 1975 the life expectancy of blacks increased by approximately three years, and the gap between whites narrowed by at least one year. There has also been a sharp decline in the proportion of elderly blacks who are widowed. Some scholars have concluded that although the economic gap between most elderly blacks and whites has narrowed since 1970, the incomes of elderly blacks are still only two-thirds of the incomes of their white counterparts. And due to unrelenting, record inflation, elderly blacks continue to pay disproportionate shares of their income for food, shelter, and other necessities. Despite these economic inequities, elderly blacks will probably continue to close the gap in income and economic status (Hill, 1978).

HISTORIC AND CONTEMPORARY ROLES

It has been long believed that the black elder has had and continues to have a particular role in the black society and society at large. The images that come forth are often stereotypical notions derived from the past and still tarnished by legend and mythology. For example, the average citizen tends to believe that the older black male is not traditionally a part of the family structure. The average older black man, many people assume, has spent a considerable part of his life running away from his responsibilities, and has no desire to support his nuclear or extended family.

In reality, during slave times, many black men either were taken away from their families or died at a very early age from illness. Many others were killed or died of plain exhaustion. Furthermore, many older black men have been responsible for rearing youngsters who were not their biological children, and many have been responsible for providing continuity for family units across generational lines. Elderly black men have traditionally felt the responsibility of caring for children in need if they were within their environmental program.

Throughout the decades, the elderly black woman has lived with many stereotypes. She has been seen as the backbone of the black community and family. She has also been looked at as the person most likely to provide wisdom and comfort to the younger generation. But in addition to these positive myths or stereotypes, there is the notion that older black women are overly absorbed in the "mammy role." It is very difficult for many elderly white persons to overcome the stereotypical notion that the only things a black woman is useful for are her sexual and domestic qualities. To allay that stereotype one only has to look at the strong leadership roles black elderly women have taken over the years. They have been responsible for many of the strides blacks have made throughout history. Black women have traditionally had higher educational levels than most black men. Even those who have not had higher formal education, such as Harriet Tubman, were successful in leading blacks at a time when there was a cry for strong leadership from anyone who would assume that responsibility.

Who cares for the older black person? The overwhelming belief that blacks generally take care of the older people in their families and communities is not always true. The fact is that not all older blacks become burdensome and represent a drain on the family resources. Actually, black elders tend to remain actively engaged in family activities as long as they are physically capable. And a reciprocal role is played by the black elders in that they are willing to give as much to a caring family as they possibly can. Over the years they have provided cohesiveness for the family by giving both material and religious support to their children, grandchildren, and often great-grandchildren. Through them the family history and folklore are passed on through the generations.

We sometimes scoff at the notion that the older black is seen as the eccentric "medicine person" in the family; however, it is true that many older blacks have the unique capability of using folk medicines very effectively. Their home remedies and herbal cures have been successful for many years. There is documented evidence that some of the herbal remedies have been successful when modern medicine has not.

At another level, it is important for the aged blacks to know that the values, norms, and skills of their generation are passed on to the very young and the young adults. It is usually the elders who perpetuate the understanding of what is wrong, what is right, and what the expected behavior and religious beliefs are.

Conflict between the traditional and modern accepted ways of doing things quite often causes confusion for young children when being raised by both parents and grandparents. These conflicts are difficult to resolve because of the desire of the young adult to honor the views of the black elder. It is not uncommon for members of the family to take sanctions against the young adult who advises or permits children to do things that do not coincide with the views of the black elder. There is a tremendous desire for the unique skills of both the elder female and male to be passed on to the younger generations, but many of the skills traditionally cherished by the older folks have been slipping away.

Traditional roles for the older black have centered around the idea of extended family but have not taken into account the reorganization of the black family into the nuclear unit. As blacks become more urbanized, it is evident that there is tension between the traditional and the expected contemporary or Anglo-oriented roles. We have been warned that the family system for blacks may suffer many uncertainties as black families take on more middle-class characteristics (Hill, 1978).

Cohesion and solidarity are two common traits of traditional extended black families that have transcended both households and special distance (Huling, 1978). It is thought that this is best attributed to the family's need to survive in all-white or nearly all-white environments that strictly reserve social and economic benefits for themselves. Blacks are, at this point, beginning to realize some of the benefits of the many battles that have been fought to have blacks recognized as viable and responsible members of our society. This will, no doubt, have an impact on many blacks as they grow older. The contemporary black person potentially represents a counterpart to blacks a generation older.

There are many things that must be considered in relation to those blacks who are now moving toward old age. The first consideration is that there are more opportunities in several areas than their parents or grandparents had. The most frightening change is the number of middle-aged blacks who are out of immediate contact with the traditional family. They have more mobility, and the value orientations of middle-aged and younger blacks seem to be changing. The lack of continuous deep personal interaction between the generations is the primary reason for some of the changes that are taking place. It is not that there is an absence of the will to be involved or to understand the values and concepts of the older generations. Voluntary mobility and more opportunities to compete in the labor market away from traditional black communities are basic reasons for the erosion of many values and beliefs.

STEREOTYPES

Considerable discussion has centered around the degree to which stereotypes and myths color our thinking of older people. The problem is perhaps more significant when one considers the role and status of the minority older person in today's world. Increasing numbers of persons are beginning to reject some of the negative stereotypes associated with the aged.

Dr. Clark Tibitts (1978) in his Donald P. Kent Memorial Lecture in 1978 discussed some of the issues around stereotypes of the aged. He contends that during the past 30 to 40 years the American society has been transforming itself from one in which older people have been held in increasingly low esteem and characterized by multiple derogative stereotypes to one in which the roles and life-styles will be increasingly viewed in a more realistic and positive manner. He further asserts that the transformation will move at a deliberate pace because (1) institutionalized negative concepts and values will change slowly; (2) the deteriorations of advanced age and the prospect of final withdrawal will continue to be viewed negatively; and (3) longer life and the resulting growing numbers of aged persons will increase the number of elderly people who manifest many of the circumstances that have given credence to negative stereotyping. It is incumbent upon scholars in the field of aging to look very closely at the elements that exist in the older population. Upon close examination one will clearly see, first, that the majority of the older population is a healthy and functioning group that contributes to our society, and second, that there are those who have varying physical, mental, or social disabilities and who display characteristics that coincide with some of these stereotypes. The emphasis has been on the 5% or less who manifest the negative stereotypes, rather than on those who are being neglected precisely because they are healthy and functioning beings and capable of and willing to contribute to our society.

The primary reason for raising the issue of stereotypes in this article is that the stereotypes normally attributed to the average older person seem to be attributed even more often to minority older persons. They are frequently seen as noncreative, very slow thinkers, and persons who cannot continue to grow and learn and be a contributing functional being.

Most of these stereotypes do not fit the character or the will of many minority older persons. Close examination shows that most minority older people in our communities continue to be involved out of necessity. It seems quite contradictory that many scholars continue to espouse the notion that minority older people remain with the family and in the community and must be responsible for themselves, and at the same time see them as noncontributing, nonfunctioning beings. It is important for the minority elder to be viewed as a positive force within his or her community. It is true that their health status and health history may not be as sound as that of their Anglo cohort, and this factor may distort the view that outsiders have of the minority older person.

One of the elements that contributes to the transition of minority older persons is that they have had a tendency to continue to be involved in the functioning of the family and the community. Out of necessity, they have had to respond to emergencies within the family or in the community because there has been no one else to respond to family needs. The stereotype of disinterest and noninvolvement certainly does not hold. Many minority older persons have had a history of being responsible and taking leadership in the community and in the family, and it seems that this tradition continues and is being strengthened. It is being strengthened primarily through the encouragement that many have gotten to become more involved in political and social arenas. Historically, many have been reluctant to become involved in the aforementioned areas. Nevertheless, many have become more involved as learners and have taken great pride in participating in a variety of programs and activities.

Summary

Despite the advances made in serving the elderly and the involvement of the elderly in determining their own destiny, a tremendous challenge remains. Black elders have taken considerable leadership in helping to shape their future. Contrary to historical patterns, they are speaking out and are investing themselves in ensuring that the appropriate mechanisms are in place to lead to their support as they grow older. A significant aspect of the transition phase for older minorities is that they are now realizing that they are not impotent. Their voices can continue to be heard and their actions will be noticed. In essence, they have become a social force to deal with.

The black elderly have participated in helping others focus on local and national priorities that will involve them. The important perspective at this juncture is to move beyond the level of priority setting. An essential next step is to begin to set into motion the agreed upon priorities that lead to a better quality of life. Physical and material needs are not the only concerns. There is a glaring need to improve the "life satisfaction" of the black aged (Chunn, 1978). The emotional and psychological well-being of the black aged has traditionally been of little or no concern to anyone. Only a dedicated few laymen and practitioners are beginning to recognize the great need for assisting the black and minority aged to deal with their emotional and psychological health and well-being. More older people have come to the realization that religion is needed, but is not necessarily the only ultimate answer to their emotional, physical, and social concerns.

The black elderly will continue to be in transition for several years. Continuous involvement in the mainstream and a sense of self-worth and pride will aid them in being more recognized as a meaningful force in the larger society. More are accepting the challenge willingly and with a fine sense of purpose. With some of the merging social policies and reinforcements, there is a much greater chance that the black elder will continue to emerge as a vital force in our society. The older black person has been quietly serving as a pillar of strength in the American society through the years, and it appears that this will be true for years to come.

REFERENCES

Chunn, J. The black aged and social policy. In *Aging*, U.S. Department of Health, Education and Welfare, Administration on Aging, Nos. 287–288, September–October 1978.

Frazer, E. F. *The negro family in the United States*. Chicago: University of Chicago Press, 1939, Chapter VIII.

Hill, R. B. A demographic profile of the black elderly. In *Aging*, U.S. Department of Health, Education and Welfare, Administration on Aging, Nos. 287–288, and T.P. 2–9, September–October 1978.

Huling, W. E. Evolving family roles for the black elderly. In *Aging*, U.S. Department of Health, Education and Welfare, Administration on Aging, Nos. 287–288, September–October 1978.

Latham, E. *The group basis of politics*. New York: Octagon Books, 1965.

Lindsay, I. *Multiple hazards of age and race: The situation of aged blacks in the U.S.* A report for the U.S. Senate Special Committee on Aging, November 12, 1971.

National Urban League. *Double jeopardy*. New York, National Urban League, 1964.

Simmons, L. *Role of the aged in primitive society*. New Haven: Yale University Press, 1945.

Stanford, E. P. Community organizations and minority aged. *The Urban League News*, 1975, 5, No. 2, April.

Tibbitts, C. Can we invalidate negative stereotypes of aging? *The Gerontologist*, 1978, *19*, 1.

U.S. Bureau of the Census. Characteristics of the population below the poverty level: 1976. Current population reports, series P-16, No. 115, 1978b.

U.S. Bureau of the Census. Estimates of the population of the U.S. by age, sex and race: 1970–1977. Current population reports, series P-25, No. 721, January 9, 1978.

U.S. Bureau of the Census. Money income in 1976 of families and persons in the U.S. Current population reports, series P-20, No. 114, 1978c.

U.S. Public Health Service, National Center for Health Statistics. Final mortality statistics, 1976. *Monthly vital statistics report*. Volume 26, No. 12, supplement 2, 1978.

Chapter 2

CULTURE AND AGING

Life-styles and Inter-generational relationships

Robert C. Atchley

Culture is the way of life of a people that is handed down from generation to generation. It influences people's language and thought, their habitual way of meeting their needs, and their physical and social environments. Culture consists mainly of ideas about how things are, how things ought to be, and how to get things done. In short, culture influences just about every aspect of human life. As a result, it is a difficult topic to relate to other complex topics, such as aging or intergenerational relationships, because it is so broad. This limitation should be kept in mind throughout this chapter.

We will begin with a view of how culture in American society influences human lives both through its impact on life in general, and in particular through its impacts on human aging and intergenerational relations. We will consider how various cultural, personal, and situational factors combine to influence life-styles. Next, we will discuss cultural and personal factors involved in adjustments to life changes. Then we will be in a position to consider various intergenerational issues and how they are influenced by cultural factors.

CULTURE AS CONTEXT

Culture is first and foremost the *context* within which individual and family life-styles are formed. It is the complex of ideas about how to live that people have created, refined, modified, and transmitted over countless generations. It consists of knowledge, beliefs, values, language, norms, laws, and the material outgrowths of these ideas.

Values tell us the relative desirability of various goals, beliefs tell us the nature of the reality in which these values are pursued, and norms tell us what we can or cannot do in the process. These ideas are related to our predispositions to *like* one thing rather than its opposite, to *expect* one thing rather than another, or to *approve of* one thing rather than another.

These values, beliefs, norms, and predispositions constantly interact with ideas about how society is or should be organized and how it operates or ought to operate. Thus the general values of society are translated into *social institutions* such as the economy, government, the family, the arts, and so forth. Social institutions operate to the extent that *groups* of people organize to pursue the goals appropriate to each institution. Groups are made up of *positions* to which various rights and duties (social roles) are attached. *Pluralistic* societies allow variations in how groups define the goals of institutions. Thus in our society corporations and labor unions are allowed to hold different views of the priorities to be served by the economic system.

Culture provides direction on how people are matched up with positions in various kinds of groups. For example, jobs are usually *achieved* by training and experience, while positions in families are *assigned* by birth or adoption.

Culture also provides conceptions of the life course—idealized biographies that give people starting points for planning and understanding the *sequence* of positions they are expected to occupy as they mature.

Obviously culture influences just about every aspect of people's lives because it is their basic mental tool kit for adapting to their environments. Culture tends to change in response to changes in the environment, but cultural change usually lags behind environmental change, and some aspects of culture can lag behind more than others.

How aging and intergenerational relations are perceived by people thus depends on the *cultural context* in which the perceiving takes place. The cultural context in the United States has certainly changed in recent years and in ways that have affected how both aging and intergenerational relations are perceived. Unfortunately, this is not the sort of subject that lends itself to quantitative data collection by the Bureau of the Census. As a result, our "knowledge" in this area consists of a sometimes interesting and sometimes infuriating amalgam of opinion, bits and pieces of "data," and only sometimes informed observations. What follows are some of my ideas. I like them, but their truth depends on whether they stand up when people try to use them.

Although negative evaluations of aging and old age have been around at least since the time of Aristotle and have been found even in societies that supposedly revered their elder members, negativity about aging and the aged has fluctuated across time and across cultures (Hendricks & Hendricks, 1977–1978; Laslett, 1977; Nahemow & Adams, 1974). Therefore, I would like to suggest that ageism is not a permanent or necessary aspect of American culture, but instead one that arose out of specific social conditions (Atchley, 1977).

When 65 was established as the minimum age for retirement under Social Security, there was an *implication* that 65 was the age at which a person might become physically or mentally too old to work. This implication occurred because, at the time Social Security was enacted, the only socially acceptable reason for retirement in American culture was the inability to continue working. That retirement might be preferred to employment was not conceivable to most Americans at that time. Also, in the early days, retirement benefit levels were so low that retirement, and by implication aging, was equated in the public mind with poverty and the life-style poverty produces. Thus both functional incapacity for work and the social stigma of poverty came to be associated with the age 65, the minimum age for retirement.

Retirement has come a long way since the 1930s. The cohort of workers who retired in 1975 averaged levels of retirement benefits that matched what the Bureau of Labor Statistics estimated as necessary to support a middle-class life-style. Retirement changed in the public mind from something one did only if one must to something one did as soon as possible. By 1975 the general public was very favorable about retirement.

As the minimum age of eligibility for retirement dropped and the general health of the older population improved, the mental link between retirement and ill health became even more absurd. By 1977 American workers were having none of the professional community's scare propaganda about the "evils" of retirement. Not an inconsiderable force in this shift was a growing retired population whose generally high levels of physical, financial, and psychological well-being put the retirement myths in perspective.

While retirement is slowly shedding its negative image, ageism in the economy is also under attack. In 1978 the Age Discrimination in Employment Act was amended to raise the mandatory retirement age to 70 and to eliminate it in some cases. Sheppard and Rix (1977) suggested that economic necessities of the future may cause the *minimum* retirement age to go up too.

The point of all this is that our attitudes and beliefs about older workers depend a lot on the economic context of the times. During labor shortages the value of older workers is extolled (McFarland, 1973; Palmore, 1975; Phillipson, nd), but in times of economic recession or labor surplus, age discrimination is frequently used to cut down the size of the labor force (Parnes & King, 1977; Sheppard, 1970).

The rise of concern over individual rights in general in our culture has allowed mandatory retirement rules to be modified. But this happened also in part because mandatory retirement rules actually affected only a tiny portion (around 7%) of the work force (Schulz, 1976).

Thus current cultural trends have produced two contradictory forces: On the one hand, high unemployment in recent years has promoted age discrimination in employment. And on the other hand, rising concern for individual rights has changed mandatory retirement policies and increased pressure for enforcement of the Age Discrimination in Employment Act.

On balance it appears that the cultural context in which older people live has improved substantially in recent years. The dramatic rise in the purchasing power of Social Security Retirement pensions, the maturing of private pension systems, and the enactment of Supplemental Security Income have greatly improved the financial situation. To be old is no longer to be poor. Living conditions have also been improved by the greater availability of low-rent housing for the elderly, transportation services, meal programs, and a host of other services. Medicare assumed a great share of the financial burden of health care for the elderly. Certainly there are still many areas that leave considerable room for improvement, but there is no denying that substantial improvement has already occurred.

These general cultural trends have improved matters not only for older people, but for their families as well. Plainly stated, the burden of support for older Americans fell on the family before 1965. And most families simply did not have the financial resources necessary to solve the income, housing, and health care problems of their older members. In my opinion, the assumption of this financial burden by society at large has freed thousands of families to concentrate on the social and emotional needs of their older members, and this too has improved the lot of both older people and their families.

These brief comments provide only a glimpse into what can be learned from looking at overall cultural trends and how they influence aging. In addition to influencing or providing the societal context in which aging and intergenerational relations take place, culture also greatly influences the specific situational context in which individuals live. It does this through its impact on life-style.

CULTURAL IMPACTS ON LIFE-STYLES

Culture provides many stock solutions to the problem of meeting human needs. Sometimes the selection of alternatives is resolved by assigning people to positions. Sometimes it is resolved by individuals themselves who must consider both the alternatives and the social pressures associated with each of them and come to an individual decision.

Literally millions of decisions are made in everyday life.

Admittedly, most of them are trivial, but some are not. To cut down the time we spend making decisions, we seek to stabilize and regularize life by developing a life-style, which in turn *implies* the resolution of many everyday dilemmas.

Life-styles are made up of living arrangements, activities (including a job), routines, patterns of dress and speech, and patterns of interaction. These various dimensions of life-style are expected to be highly compatible. Choices about life-styles are influenced by a number of factors, including both general and age-specific values and norms, the life course, personal preferences, and the processes society uses to locate people in groups and positions. Life-style choices are also influenced by subcultural forces such as sex, social class, race or ethnicity, region of the country, and urban versus rural residence.

In the context of the general social conditions of the time and place we live in, life-style is the most important aspect of life for most people. Decisions about what sort of job to take, where to live, with whom to live, whether to have children, whether to go to college (or back to college), what to buy, what to do, and countless others depend on our having at least a basic overview of the sort of life we would like to lead—our preferred life-style.

Most Americans select a "traditional" life-style that involves long-term employment in one's eventual occupation, or long-term commitment to being a housewife, to marriage, parenthood, residence in an independent household, a diverse pattern of activities, residential stability near family members, and daily, weekly, and yearly routines structured around the demands of jobs, marriage, housekeeping, parenthood, and family responsibilities. Although there are numerous exceptions, most middle-aged Americans find themselves in life-styles that generally fit this description. Once people are established in a life-style, they tend to keep it if possible.

Culture, Life Course Events, and Life-styles

Life course events are the main causes of life-style changes in later adulthood. Some life course events can be anticipated and some cannot, but most such events offer an opportunity to rethink the appropriateness of one's life-style and change it accordingly. For example, having launched the children gives a couple a chance to develop new activities and routines. Retirement frees life-styles from the external constraints imposed by job schedules. Both of these changes can be anticipated and planned for.

On the other hand, widowhood often forces people to accept what is to them a less desirable life-style—living alone. Interestingly, our research has indicated that most people can weather the empty nest and retirement with only minor adjustments in life-styles. Life-styles can be adapted quickly to even such profound events as widowhood, provided the person has an adequate income and good health. Those who change life-styles in response to life course events either choose to change or have change imposed on them by an overbearing family member.

The major exception to this general rule is institutionalization. Life in institutions is usually so drastically different from life in the community that only rarely can existing life-styles be adapted to handle the change. In addition, the person's resources for adapting are usually reduced by illness, disability, or both. As a result, most people who move to institutions must develop an entirely new life-style and one in which their choices are limited. In my opinion this change, more than worries about poor care, is the root of the prevailing fear older people have about entering institutions, as well as the root of the movement to keep older persons in their customary households as long as possible.

INTERGENERATIONAL RELATIONS

Intergenerational relations thus occur in a cultural context that includes ideas about the aged, intergenerational responsibilities, the ideal life course, appropriate responses to life course changes, life-styles, and how life-styles are affected by aging and by life course changes. Again, all of these factors can vary by social class, race or ethnicity, region of the country, and urban versus rural residence.

Relationships between generations occur most often in a family context. Accordingly, we will now consider some of the issues involved in generational relations and how these issues are affected by cultural factors. This discussion will center around interactions between adult children and their older parents. The issues to be considered can be grouped into those that concern family solidarity and those that concern the family's response to adversity.

As most introductory sociology students learn, groups are held together by two types of forces: agreement on ideas and division of labor. There is great potential for conflict in families over values, norms, beliefs, and knowledge. In a world where social change is rapid, the experiences one generation uses to arrive at their personal attitudes, values, and beliefs can be quite different from those of another generation. Fortunately, because most members of both generations select "traditional" life-styles, there is less intergenerational differences than might be supposed. In fact, Troll and Bengtson (1978) reviewed the literature and found a great deal of intergenerational similarity with respect to values and norms. They also found that children tend to select friends who reinforce the values they learned from their parents. The only area where there seemed to be a noticeable differential between generations was in ideas about sex roles. And even when there was disagreement it did not seem to interfere with interaction between generations. Somehow, the parent-child bond generally seems able to tolerate more disagreement than one would expect.

The division of labor in adult child–older parent relations rests mainly on the responsibilities of the generations with respect to each other. Generally, each generation is responsible for meeting its own needs unless health, disability, or financial disaster prevents it. When these difficulties arise, aid can be expected to flow in whatever direction it is needed. Aid does not merely flow toward older parents; it may come from them as well. The evidence overwhelmingly supports the notion that when family members need aid, they get it, and this is particularly true for the older generations. The family's response to older members holds true regardless of whether there are strong ties of affection between generations (Troll, Miller, & Atchley, 1979). Lozier and Althouse (1974) have pointed out that this bond is partly the result of fear of negative public opinion should one fail to live up to the canons of filial duty set forth in the culture.

Various forms of adversity can befall older people and their families. Older members can become unemployed before they retire. Older couples with handicapped adult children can expect their parental responsibilities to continue into retirement or widowhood. Middle-aged persons can find themselves squeezed by dependency needs of both their children and their parents. Yet the strong family values in our society seem to carry families through diversity. And recent social programs have made it much easier for families to meet the needs of their older members.

In summary, there can be no doubt that ageism is a negative force in the lives of many older people. Yet many have life-styles that are scarcely affected by ageism, and the value put on individual rights and equity in our society has supported program changes that have greatly improved conditions for the elderly.

American families have generally cared for their own. However, as the population aged, the financial burden of this care exceeded the capacities of many families. Fortunately, the recently improved economic conditions of the elderly have put the family back in business.

And the family is only one of many resources older people have. Most older people have developed stable life-styles that are flexible enough to accommodate most life course changes. Adequate income and health are great assets. So are energy and a nimble mind. Fortunately, most older people are able to cope with aging adequately with the tools they develop themselves and with those they learn from their culture. Certainly our culture does not hand a perfect life to older people, but neither does it leave them as empty-handed as many would have us believe.

REFERENCES

Atchley, R. C. *The social forces in later life* 2nd ed. Belmont, California: Wadsworth, 1977.

Hendricks, J., & Hendricks, C. D. The age old question of old age: Was it really so much better back when? *Aging and Human Development,* 1977–1978, *8,* 139–154.

Laslett, P. Societal development and aging. In R. H. Binstock & E. Shanas (Eds.), *Handbook of aging and the social sciences.* New York: Van Nostrand Reinhold, 1977.

Lozier, J. & Althouse, R. Social enforcement of behavior toward elders in an Appalachian mountain settlement. *Gerontologist*, 1974, *14*, 69–80.

McFarland, R. A. The need for functional age measures in industrial gerontology. *Industrial Gerontology*, 1973, *1*, 1–19.

Nahemow, N. & Adams, B. N. Old age among the Boganda: Continuity and change. In J. F. Gubrim (Ed.), *Late life*. Springfield, Illinois: Charles C. Thomas, 1974.

Palmore, E. *The honorable elders*. Durham, North Carolina: Duke University Press, 1975.

Parnes, H. & King, R. Middle-aged job losers. *Industrial Gerontology*, 1977, *4*, 77–95.

Phillipson, C. *The emergence of retirement*. Durham, England: University of Durham, nd.

Schulz, J. H. *The economics of aging*. Belmont, California: Wadsworth, 1976.

Sheppard, H. L. *Industrial gerontology*. Cambridge, Massachusetts: Schenkman, 1970.

Sheppard, H. L., & Rix, S. E. *The graying of working America: The coming crisis of retirement age policy*. New York: The Free Press, 1977.

Troll, L. E., & Bengtson, V. L. Generations in the family. In W. Burr et al., (Eds.), *Contemporary theories about the family*. New York: The Free Press, 1978.

Troll, L. E., Miller, S. J., & Atchley, R. C. *Families in later life*. Belmont, California: Wadsworth, 1979.

Chapter 3

INTERGENERATIONAL PERSPECTIVES ON AGING

Irving Rosow

After decades of relative neglect, the aged have received a greater measure of attention the past few years through academic, professional, and political channels, through the media, and through the elderly themselves. This new awareness has sprung from many sources—from sober scientists to advocates as diverse as Maggie Kuhn, Robert Butler, and Hugh Downes.

Two aspects of such exposure are especially noteworthy. First, while the aged have been significant targets of this communication, basically it has addressed an intergenerational audience. Not only have the self-images and self-evaluations of the elderly been at stake—young and middle-aged people's views of the old have been at issue as well. Thus the communications involve several generations and may even mediate intergenerational relations.

Second, much of the sentiment being projected both sentimentalizes and idealizes older people. It is not enough that the aged are simply people like all others, they must also become paragons who gain strengths and qualities that they never enjoyed in middle age. The basic purpose of this idealization is to change people's attitudes, to engender in younger generations a finer appreciation of the elderly and thereby to improve their treatment and social position.

This attempt to change people's minds is based on the Madison Avenue precept that well-nigh everything, including favorable attitudes, can be successfully peddled in much the same fashion as breakfast food and detergents. Apparently, the only problem is to find the key to the successful promotion—the right gimmick, twist, or buzzword. Ostensibly the right approach can be the key to almost anything, including political careers and the White House itself.

Merchandising and politics, however, have limits; not everything is readily salable. Despite major investments and careful planning by experts, the promotions of the Edsel and Harold Stassen's several presidential candidacies were not successful. Certain qualities, some extremely subtle, may set limits on what can be promoted, and occasional firm consumer resistance reflects underlying realities that are not easily manipulated. When the buyer is wary, let the seller also beware lest he delude himself about the market potential.

The same caution applies to selling a bright new image of the aged. We can modify people's views and soften their attitudes somewhat, but this will not fundamentally change the world. Nor will wishing make it so. For the experience of aging is grounded in a set of objective circumstances in which the sentiments of younger generations are not terribly important. Indeed, our attitudes toward the aged shape our institutions less than they are shaped by them. The fate of our older people is governed essentially by factors other than our attitudes. What are some of these?

The primary reality in the intergenerational relations of older persons is social loss of roles, functions, resources, power, and position—in other words those aspects of life that had conferred their social identity (what they were), their place in the social order (where they were), and their claim on its rewards (how they made out).

This loss is clearly reflected in the changes that overtake the generation over the age of 65. Perhaps this group can be best described as one whose members are constantly replaced, when they die, by new recruits who have just reached 65. Nonetheless, even though its members are constantly passing through and changing the composition of the group, its characteristics remain surprisingly stable—shifting slowly in accordance with social change. Now, what are the main social losses that appear after 65?

First, there is the general decline in health. While the newly aging generation and the next one on the horizon may prove to be slightly less afflicted than their predecessors, their pattern of health change is similar. Chronic illness sets in as people grow older, and most of them come to live tolerably well with its inconvenience, discomfort, or pain. Fortunately, serious incapacity is limited to only a minority of the aged. Of those over 65, about one in seven (15%) is bed-bound, housebound, or severely restricted in mobility. The proportion is lower for those under 75 and higher for those older, because chronic conditions generally increase and get worse with the passing years. For the age group as a whole, however, the proportion with severe health problems has remained at the remarkably stable figure of 15% for several decades. At the same time, we must appreciate that while the other 85% are managing fairly well, the overall course of their health is declining—and some will join those handicapped 15%.

The decline in health has several implications for old persons' social relations: (1) With greater disability, there is a sharp increase in dependence and its associated problems of care and financing. (2) Even for those not so restricted, life space, both within and between generations, contracts. Old people simply move through a smaller physical and social world. (3) The full energy and competence that normal adult roles presuppose must be validated. In dealing with those under 65, adequate health is usually expected, and any limitations require some special allowances to be made. For those over 65, adequate health cannot routinely be assumed, but must be evaluated. To the extent that old people's health cannot simply be taken for granted as adequate for adult roles, it becomes problematic in intergenerational contexts.

A second major loss in old age especially for women, is loss of a spouse. Of those people over 65, more than one-half of the women and 15% of the men are widowed. Needless to say, widowhood rises sharply with age. Among men it increases from less than one-tenth of those under 75 to one-fourth of those older. And among women it rises from two-fifths of those under 75 to two-thirds of those older.

Trends of the past 20 years have increased the difference between the sexes. The proportion of widowed women has remained fairly constant, but widowhood among men has declined by about one-third. Women's life expectancy has increased faster than men's, so more men stay husbands and fewer become widowers. Consequently, the incidence of widowhood among men has gone down. The slight overall drop in widowhood for all older persons has benefited more husbands than wives. Demographers expect this trend to continue, with more wives outliving husbands and surviving afterwards for longer periods. Since a woman's social position is still controlled mainly by marriage and her husband's occupation, widowhood introduces many uncertainties into her relations, not only with peers, but with other generations as well.

Another major role loss is retirement. It affects both men and working women, but it is almost always a focal problem for men. As our economy has grown in size and complexity over the years, the proportion of older men still in the work force has declined steadily. Now fewer than one-fourth of the men over 65 work at all, and only about one in seven works full time. Very few old women, well under 10%, are now employed or have been in recent decades.

Retirement increases not only with age and poor health, but with several other factors as well. For both men and women, continued employment is directly related to education and occupational level. Generally, the better educated and those in higher occupations work longer; the less educated and those in lower occupations do not.

Improvements in retirement income and loosening values about work and leisure have increased voluntary and early retirement, although the extreme inflation of the 1970s has almost certainly slowed this trend and deprived it of the force it was gathering. Nonetheless, insofar as occupation is still the key to social class and social identity, retirement remains a consequential role loss. Six of seven men over 65 no longer work full-time, in contrast to approximately 10% of younger men. For older men such loss of work reduces their authority in intergenerational relationships.

For many persons, old age is the adult life stage when they experience their lowest income. Several correlates of age, such as retirement or widowhood, depress income, while others, such as sex or race, magnify previous income differentials. It is difficult to document properly the inadequacy of old people's current income. The lag in publication of recent data and the rapid rate of inflation make fresh government figures resemble quaint historical anecdotes. The general pattern, however, is apparent.

The income disadvantage of the elderly is clear in many respects. Depending on occupation and education, earnings reach their peak sometime between 35 and 55, and then decline. They hold up slightly better for women who continue to work than for men. Overall, older workers generally earn significantly less than those who are younger. Furthermore, upon retirement, income for both men and women is reduced to less than one-half of what it was while they were working. This drop is reflected in the poverty rate. One-sixth of those over 65 subsist below the official poverty threshold, which is by far the highest proportion of any adult age group.

Among the elderly, former income differences between the races, the sexes, and the married versus the unmarried are increased. Thus the relative income disadvantages become even larger for old blacks and other minorities, for women, and for single persons. Among the unrelated, single men have more income than single women—most of them widows. By and large, minority widows who live alone are at the bottom of the income barrel.

Different combinations of several factors (sex, race, family status, marital status, employment) show between 5 and 55% of various subgroups below the poverty threshold. Insofar as most older persons are retired, severe inflation makes their real income shrink rapidly. Pegging social security to the Consumer Price Index does not Sanforize the monthly check; it sets in motion a catch-up game in which the old person is extremely vulnerable.

The reduction of income has both intrinsic and symbolic meaning. The immediate effects of lower living standards are echoed in the social losses that they signify. Consumption patterns are basic to life-styles and status. So a major loss of income that reduces living standards and may even risk downward mobility is in itself invidious. The ancillary losses include membership in organizations and informal groups, and losses in entertaining, travel, and other activities that reflect social position but can no longer be afforded. The results are real and symbolic losses in living standards, affiliations, and life-styles.

The loss of roles takes two different forms. The first is reduction in the number of roles that a person performs, as exemplified by retirement. The person leaves work, loses his position in the labor force, and no longer does a job. So the work role is lost. The same thing happens when a person drops out of a group or organization or loses any other position that is not replaced. In the second form of loss, the role itself shrinks. The position is not lost, but its time, activity, and content are reduced. This contraction of the role is not uncommon. It is exemplified in the successive stages of parenthood through the life course as children grow up, become adults, establish families, and raise their own children. One remains a parent throughout these developments, but the content of the role contracts. As children attain progressive degrees of independence and self-sufficiency, parents have sharply reduced obligations and activities.

Older people are subject to both kinds of role attrition: reduction in the *number* of roles and *shrinkage* of their content. Both are involved in the decline in old people's social participation.

The increase in retirement and widowhood, and the decline in health and income also signify people's growing social obsolescence, for they invariably involve reduction of responsibility and functions that have a significant effect on others. Although there are notable exceptions among older executives, political officials, professionals, and others who have been able to retain positions of power and authority, they are in the minority. For the age group as a whole, responsibility, authority, and control are reduced, and the scope of their functions, activity, and influence diminishes sharply.

Such social obsolescence is real, not simply a figment of imagination or stereotyping. To be sure, some of it may reflect swiftly changing fashions, so that the next Andy Warhol in the artistic firmament might be a burnt-out relic by the age of 27 as new fads replace his or her style. Other bases of influence and regard, however, are not so capricious. Other things being equal, the hotshot young physicist of 25 necessarily has more contribution ahead of him than he will have left at 45 or than his ex-hotshot teacher of 45 still has left. This is simply the whiz kid syndrome in periods of rapid social change. Such rapid change in a complex society only underscores how quickly prime competence may pass from one generation to the next.

Under present conditions, experts of 20 and even 10 years ago are no longer leaders or authorities in many areas. Not only in the rapidly changing fields of hard science and technology, but also in softer spheres that are changing equally rapidly: athletics, law, social policy, architecture, music, journalism, sex roles, psychotherapy, literature, child rearing, merchandising, and life-styles. Research has shown a great deal more familial and intergenerational continuity in many vital spheres than most youthful rebellion would lead us to expect. But this is not the whole story, for significant discontinuities are developing in the areas of greatest change. What is moot is not different generational styles or idioms, but more basic values. It is not simply that many young physicians are hip dressers, but that so many more of them are convinced of the need for socialized medicine. In this vein, how many of today's young adults regard their parents or their parents' contemporaries as reliable authorities-confidants-consultants, much less models, in resolving their own existential dilemmas—especially in such newly problematic spheres as appropriate sex roles, parenthood, careers, religion, life-styles, and the proper claims of the Protestant Ethic? The net result of *significant* social change is to weaken the moral authority of the older generation over the younger.

We have discussed the loss of roles that systematically overtakes older people, and we have linked this to their social obsolescence. Whatever old people's personal qualities, they tend to be depreciated and shunted aside because they seem to be dispensable in our social system. And sometimes this idea that they are dispensable becomes a self-fulfilling prophecy. They are diverted from the mainstream of social activity to peripheral spheres, often local cul-de-sacs. When they are shunted to inconsequential positions, they are then regarded as inconsequential themselves—in that perverse confusion of cause and effect that distinguishes self-fulfilling prophecies.

But what do the decrements and obsolescence really signify? Their most important implication is that the losses are *structural*. They have an objective social basis so that they are real in the real world. They reflect not only a devaluation of the aged that pep talks and public relations campaigns try to sway; more important- ly, they entail losses of responsibility and key functions that signi- ficantly affect other people. These changes alter old people's social participation. By deflection and default, they move from central involvement in the major institutions to marginal posi- tions. Old people's social functions decline and become peripher- al. This is the reason that one of the founding patriarchs of gerontology regarded the role of the elderly as vacuous. Ernest Burgess termed this development the *rolelessness* of old age.

This is not to say that all the devaluation of old people has an objective base and cannot be reversed through attitude change. But it does emphasize that most of the social losses of old age are indeed objective. They are no minor aberration of how our society functions, but a direct result of our values and institutions. We are a competitive, profit-oriented modern economy with tremendously short-term perspectives. We are wedded to the principles of size, economic growth, and expanding markets. Competitive advantage is rooted in technical and scientific in- novation and in rapid adaptation to new knowledge and tech- niques. These are not simply important values in our society; they are its organizing core and motive force. Their governing princi- ples integrate our major institutions: the economy, government, education, science, religion, and the family.

From the viewpoint of the social system, rapid scientific and technological change depreciates existing skills, renders people obsolete, and limits the period of their economic value and social utility. Those resources that are critical are transmitted to the young, who contribute productively to the system but receive gradually diminishing returns into their middle age. Against this perspective, the experience, judgment, and skills of the older generations are not particularly compelling.

Hence, whatever intrinsic value older people might have, there is comparatively little *market* for them—either economic or social. The crossover point seems to correspond to that period in middle age when men and women find it hard to enter the labor market and compete successfully for better new jobs. If there is no labor shortage because of a careening expansion of the economy, the proportion of successful aspirants declines with age—by about 40 for manual workers and less than 10 years later for nonmanual positions. This means that occupational obsolescence has already arrived and a withering has begun.

This pattern of the labor market is also reflected in various social markets, for obsolescence is not solely an economic phenomenon. It is paralleled by older people's declining social utility and the reduced demand for them in many noneconomic markets. This reflects quite dispassionately where they stand, their worth and esteem in our current scheme of values.

Under these conditions, aging involves the movement toward rolelessness. Society gives little structure to old people's lives—or more accurately, their socially patterned ties with other persons gradually come apart. As roles are lost or shrink, the requirements on the elderly become tenuous and their lives lose structure. With few responsibilities or demands, there is almost nothing that they really have to do. Within the constraints of health and income, they probably have greater freedom of choice than at any other time in their lives.

This freedom seems heavenly to those in the overworked, overmortgaged, overtaxed middle generation. Exchanging our burdens for a freedom from hassle sounds as enticing as a Siren's song. But *caveat emptor*, for those limited demands are really a double-edged blessing. They increase freedom and opportunity, but they also exchange one kind of responsibility for another. Such a limitation in demands moves the individual from a world of obligation to one created by choice, from the world of imposed social norms to one of self determination. Some older persons thrive on it, but many cannot face it.

Most people's lives are shaped by several key decisions: the work they do, whether and whom they marry (or divorce), where they decide to live, when they have children and how many, how much they educate them, the church they belong to. A few other personal characteristics, such as age, sex, race, and ethnicity, round out the other main factors. These decisions and attributes trace the outline of their lives, including many basic beliefs and even their daily schedules. Bakers start work at 2 in the morning, surgeons at 6, other manual workers at 8, insurance agents at 9, and numbers runners even later. A suburban mother schedules her day around the imperatives of chauffering that do not concern a slum mother who just wants to get home for supper. The objective basis of life allows us to fill in many of these features. This is what we mean by the social structuring of life.*

Various details then fit into the framework—and these tend to be choices of consumption: the kind of car to buy, whether to give the kids music lessons, whether to borrow money or to forego the vacation to pay for the orthodontia, or whether kids that small really need training bras—the most perverse form of the mind-body problem—especially if they are just going to throw them away when they grow up. But such decisions fit into the overall life-style, whatever it might be.

When middle-aged adults grumble about being under a yoke, they are complaining about responsibilities and lives that are overdetermined. When they talk of being in a rut, they are complaining about routines that are so overstructured that possible choices don't even occur to them.

The main point here is not to specify the particular factors that shape life, but simply to recall that it has an objective basis and a structure that does govern activities and fill our time. So when most adults get up in the morning, they know what they will have to do that day. In fact, most of the day is already spoken for, and there is little room for real options.

This is a two-tier process: First, responsibilities determine functions, and then options fill out the rest of the schedule. Obligations take precedence over discretionary activities. Or in the rhetoric of another era, work before pleasure. This is the pattern of most adult life.

But old age changes this pattern as social roles diminish or disappear. Each lost role empties out a bit more of life, and when enough are lost to drastically reduce activity and contact with people, then life can become very empty indeed. To be sure, this emptiness can be moderated if old people remain securely anchored in informal networks of family and friends. Nonetheless, even with these networks, particularly if they are weak, the

---

*This idea has no relation to the symbolic interactionists' conception of the negotiated "construction of reality."

loss of social roles remains consequential. Such loss moves the aged from structured time and activity to the realm of personal choice. Even if informal networks take up some of the slack, the elderly still have to do most of the job themselves. To reclaim their emptier days, they must compensate for their losses and fill the new gaps that have begun to pockmark their lives.

These gaps may open new possibilities, and to those who can exploit it, the new freedom may present exciting opportunities. But to those who cannot, the freedom becomes a burden, if not a tyranny. The active fashioning of one's life is a supremely creative process. To fill each day and give the accumulating days a coherent, meaningful shape require self-knowledge, ingenuity, and commitment. Good judgment and deep personal resources are needed to make the appropriate choices. The entire process requires the exercise of more *continuous* responsibility for oneself than ever before. So the social losses put people on their mettle to an extent that most never experienced and that few others now appreciate.

Many older people can meet this challenge and fashion a reasonable life. On the other hand, many others cannot, and these people age in isolation and pain. In a study in Michigan some years ago, one-half the sample of old people were very bored and wanted to have some new experience, and half of these had enough money and were healthy enough to do so. When they were asked why they didn't do what they wanted, they could give no reason, only a sheepish shrug.

Similarly, in my own research, in apartments with few old residents, many of them were isolated from their younger neighbors, were very lonely, and wanted more social contact. In those buildings that had many older residents, there was a boiling social life. Nonetheless, about half as many people as in the other apartments were also isolated and lonely. This occurred under optimal conditions for neighboring.

In both these cases the solution to a problem—whether of new experience or neighboring—was at hand, but it required personal resources and initiative that a significant number of people lacked. These are the most vulnerable elderly. As they lose roles, the structure that sustained them in earlier stages grows faint, and they do not have the means to compensate and reorder their lives by themselves.

So when psychologists naively wonder why role loss is important so long as people are happy, this is the answer: Many are not. Most people are sufficiently developed and resourceful to withstand loss. But many others, at least a substantial minority, lack certain personal qualities. The social system had previously set most of their norms and expectations so that they did not have to create the basic structure of their lives. The price of any limited training or personal deficiency was neither immobilizing nor exorbitant. However, if they experience major social losses in old age, they are then in a predicament. They must reconstruct their lives on their own, and they are unable to do this effectively. Thus role loss not only places a premium on the informal supports of the elderly, but also magnifies the importance of their personal resources, capacities, and imagination.

This analysis has considered the basis and some consequences of older people's marginal social position. This position is rooted in the objective conditions of their lives and is not simply a function of the insensitivity and prejudice of younger persons. Consequently, any efforts to improve the circumstances of the elderly cannot be significant if they focus on changing intergenerational attitudes without reference to the objective factors that govern the fate of the aged. Such factors have not proved particularly pliant in the past.

While the future for older persons may be darkening, in general, the opportunities for objective social functioning may revive during the next several decades. In a purely historical perspective, it is likely that the age of affluence has crested and that we are already in the transition to future eras of basic scarcity. Quite apart from the crises of oil and energy, we have entered a period of steadily rising costs that will reflect deepening scarcities and may ultimately wreck modern advanced economies. Certainly in the short run of the next few decades, and accelerating after that, I expect trends of continuing inflation; slowing economic growth; reduced capital formation; selective, but declining capital investment; increasing disruption and strain in the coordination of national economies; massive technological crises; drastically reduced productivity; and probably the disintegration of advanced technologies. I am not invoking Buck Rogers and the technocrats, but George Orwell and Robert Heilbroner. For I do not expect a technological miracle to rescue us from this looming crisis. We are in for hard times, very hard times, for everybody. This will be a world that nobody made, but nobody prevented. Yet the relative losses of old people may not be as extreme as those of the middle-aged and the young.

The key to these developments lies in our declining productivity and the eventual reversion to a less capital-intensive technology. If we are not able to sustain our present level of industrialization, then our productivity must inevitably decline. In 2020, 5% of the population will not feed the other 95%. This would be true in all enterprises and sectors in which technological levels cannot be advanced or even maintained.

Under these conditions, a simpler form of economy must inevitably emerge, one based on lower capitalization, simpler equipment, and a lower output of the system and all its components. Given lower productivity, the marginal output of each worker declines. Thus a larger number of workers is needed to maintain a given population, even at reduced living standards. This means that as marginal productivity falls, the importance of each worker rises—not in terms of his high production and wages, but simply for his marginal utility. Scarcity and low productivity combine to increase the need and market for older workers and their marginal yield. Thus, low productivity preserves the objective functions and social roles of the aged, thereby integrating them into the social order.

This process should be augmented by two factors. First, whatever other changes the next few decades might bring, high costs should drastically slow scientific and technological development. So the value of older people's knowledge and skills should last longer. This should significantly reduce the rate at which the aged become obsolete, certainly in the labor force if nowhere else. If there is a premium on technically uncomplicated solutions to production or economic problems, the elderly might be at little disadvantage.

Second, the costs of retirement income (and most other social programs) will prove prohibitive and unsupportable in an economy of scarcity. While there may well be unemployment, which will not help the aged, there should be little retirement as we know it for reasons other than illness. The recent lifting of mandatory retirement provisions is but a harbinger of things to come.

What we may face in the first part of the twenty-first century is an economy with many elements from the nineteenth, features of early and pre-industrialization. The place of the elderly in that social order should be closer to what it was a century ago than to what it is now. While there will be austerity, turbulence, and considerable competition for scarcities, age should not be the primary basis of conflict. So long as we can achieve a reasonable state of equilibrium and control without wild gyrations, even with a simpler, less technical economy, the social structure should accommodate and integrate several adult generations fairly well. But we need not venture to peer beyond the first part of the twenty-first century.

Chapter 4

THE CONTINUUM OF LIVING ARRANGEMENTS

Traditional, Novel, and Pragmatic Alternatives*

Gordon F. Streib

Interest in the aged and in gerontological studies has grown enormously in the last decade. One of the gaps in our knowledge and in our array of services for the elderly are alternative living arrangements, especially for the frail, the slightly impaired, and others who need some sort of sheltered housing but do not need nursing care. Almost everyone in the aging field is aware of the concept that there is a continuum of living arrangements ranging from living independently in one's own house to complete institutionalization, with 24-hour-a-day skilled nursing care provided.

This awareness that there must be a variety of living arrangements to meet the needs of the older population is related to the heterogeneity of America's elderly, who differ in income, family arrangements, level of health, mobility, and attitudes and personality. However, the diversity of the elderly does not mean we

*Supported in part by grants from the Andrus Foundation—NRTA-AARP, Washington, DC, and the Administration on Aging, Department of Health, Education and Welfare. The opinions expressed are those of the author.

cannot make generalizations about subgroups. It is well known that as the population ages, the sex ratio slowly and inexorably changes, and results in a far larger percentage of women than men. Over time, there has been an increasing disparity in the number of males versus females aged 65 and over. In 1930 there were 102 males per 100 females. In 1960 there were 82 males per 100 females, and in 1975 there were 69 males per 100 females. This disparity increases even more at older ages, so that at age 85, there are 185 women for every 100 males. Thus one of the first generalizations is that when we speak of alternative living arrangements for the elderly, we are speaking predominantly of older women.

There are many reasons why elderly people encounter problems living independently in their own homes: (1) A large number are widows and have trouble coping with upkeep of the house and property. (2) They may be left in declining neighborhoods in urban areas, and sometimes they are the victims of crime. (3) Their children and relatives who might offer assistance live in other areas. (4) The increasing number of women in the labor force means that daughters are not free to take care of elderly parents. (5) With the longer life span, it is increasingly common for people to live to their 80s and 90s, and to outlive their own children. (6) Older siblings rarely share a household, except for single or never-married persons. (7) The longer life expectancy of women, the lower income of widows, and the effects of inflation combine to increase the urgency of finding more economical housing than is possible when living alone in a single dwelling.

Housing changes are considered in about half of all disability cases, according to a nationwide survey reported by Newman (1976). The major alternatives, especially for persons over 75, are moving into the household of relatives or entering a nursing home. Traditionally, the first alternatives to be considered were for the elderly persons to move in with their children, or for the children to live with the parents. These solutions are not favored in urban America, either by the adult children or the elderly themselves. Both generations prize their freedom and independence; the older generation frequently does not want to endanger the affectional ties with their children by living with them.

Home care is another recent solution for the moderately dependent older person. Its purpose is to maintain the older person in his or her own residence as long as possible. Her needs are met by supplying housekeeping services, Meals-on-Wheels, visiting nurses, therapists, transportation, and CETA workers to make home repairs.

Supplying supportive services to permit people to remain in their homes is considered the best option by many persons in gerontology, for they regard staying in one's own home as the *top* priority. However, when many services are required, the coordination of activities becomes very complicated and the costs escalate. Furthermore, there are some important problems that cannot be solved by such means. Let me give you an example from my own community:

This case involves a widow who is struggling to remain in her home in a changing neighborhood. She has a serious heart condition and high blood pressure. Almost everyone she has known in the neighborhood for the last 30 years has moved or died. Foremost in her mind is the fear of crime—and she keeps a handgun by her bed. When asked if she would go to her son's home 30 miles away for Christmas dinner, she replied that she did not dare leave her home for that long a time for fear of being robbed. Even so, she has been robbed several times.

She gets Meals-on-Wheels but often does not care for what is served. She has homemaker services, but this is a source of great conflict—there is constant turnover in the housekeepers, and she does not like the housekeeping standards of the persons sent. They will not wash windows or clean under the bed, which distresses her greatly. Then, as a final touch of irony, one waxed her bathroom floor so excessively that she slipped and broke her ankle, ending up in a cast for two months.

She is taken for her doctor's appointments by the senior citizen minibus, but often it is late, and she is in a state of agitation by the time she gets to the physician. The housing inspectors have presented her with a list of about 20 repairs she must make or her house will be condemned. Clearly, supportive services do not solve the multiple problems of keeping this woman in her own home.

The Continuum of Living Arrangements

Housing for the elderly can be considered a continuum, ranging from living independently in one's own home to entering a full-care institution. Understanding the continuum enables one to analyze the various alternative family and living arrangements. Perhaps the most significant theoretical and policy issue is that of age segregation versus age integration. Rosow (1967) studied different degrees of age segregation in Cleveland, Ohio, and pointed to the social benefits of a residential environment that has a large number of age peers.

Other studies report high satisfaction with age-segregated living arrangements. In recent years many persons have moved to retirement communities and find them a highly satisfactory housing alternative (Jacobs, 1974; Bultena & Wood, 1969). One implication is that there is no one desirable form of retirement environment that is endorsed by all older persons, or can be recommended for all elderly. Indeed, we must always be aware that older people are socially heterogeneous, and attempts must be made to provide diverse living arrangements.

Hochschild's (1973) detailed case study of one small apartment building also offers important, confirmatory qualitative data on how age-segregated housing may produce positive results for low-income older persons. Living in a marginal urban area does not mean that older persons are isolated from their families and feel lonely, Hochschild states. She was surprised to find an unexpected sense of community in this age-homogenous housing project.

Traditional Alternative Living Arrangements

Retirement hotels are one traditional variant living arrangement. Albrecht (1969), who studied retirement hotels in Florida, found that the active, young, and independent retirees often preferred this type of housing. Health is an important consideration; in fact, some retirement hotels or clubs require a statement from a physician indicating that the individual is ambulatory and self-sufficient.

Albrecht (1969) reported that "Concern for residents is not unusual. One hotel has a breakfast roll call, others make various checks on them and sometimes neighbors, friends or buddies take care of this and report illness to the management. . . . The retirement hotels visited keep records of next of kin or others to be notified in case this is necessary" (p. 79). Thus these hotels provide services beyond those of the usual commercial hotel. Many residents prefer them because they are independent and can come and go as they please, without reporting to anyone or accounting for their activities. In addition, the food was usually good in the places studied, and the residents enjoyed the companionship and recreational facilities. However, there are potential problems if the person's physical or mental condition deteriorates, Albrecht concluded.

A slightly different picture was painted in a recent careful study by Stephens (1976) of elderly tenants in a slum hotel in a large midwestern city. She found that this type of housing seemed to be preferred by male loners who wished to avoid social involvement. Indeed, the work of Stephens emphasized that many of the older urban residents cling fiercely to their autonomy and privacy in the slum hotel, and regard it as preferable to living in any kind of an institutional setting, which might offer more services.

Two other recent studies of elderly hotel residents in Seattle and San Diego report similar findings, particularly that the residents were highly independent and self-reliant. The Seattle team (Lally, Black, Thornock, & Hawkins, 1979) reported that "They are reticent to enter dependent relationships with 'helpers' which they perceive could compromise their self concepts. They either lack contact with or under-utilize existing social services which they distrust because they believe representatives of these agencies have the power to deny them the life style of their choosing" (p. 72). In San Diego the investigators (Erickson & Eckert, 1977) found that the most effective services and social supports were those provided by the hotel staff and neighborhood shopkeepers.

Another alternative housing arrangement for the elderly, probably favored more in the past than now, is the boarding home. I shall discuss here some data from an excellent study done in Missouri under a grant for an Administration on Aging research project conducted by Ellen H. Biddle, Robert Habenstein, and Charles Mindel (Habenstein, Kieffer, & Wang, 1976). The investigators classified homes into three groups: small—two or three persons, and generally not licensed; medium—seven or eight persons; and large, up to 30 persons, which is the legal limit. All groups are run for profit, although in the marginal or smaller ones profit is often minimal; they may just break even. These homes are operated by local people in small towns, and there is often community involvement in the homes. Most families consider them a much more desirable living arrangement than nursing homes when a frail or impaired person is unable to take care of herself, or when the relatives cannot take them in. The average age of the residents is 82, and half of the older people are able to pay the charges with their own funds.

A third of all moves to boarding homes are inititated by a physician. While the decision to enter is primarily a family matter, the doctor facilitates the decision by his recommendation. Since such a decision is nearly always an unwelcome one, the physician's role is to ratify the unpleasant step that the family must take.

The Missouri boarding home situation has an interesting feature in that all residents in licensed homes need a sponsor—a responsible person concerned with the welfare of the resident. It may be more than one person, but in 60% of the cases the sponsor is a son or daughter.

The Missouri investigators reported that although the smaller boarding homes are marginal operations in buidings of lower quality, the quality of care and the amount of concern and personal attention was often higher than that observed in the larger, well-appointed homes. In 1973, when a new law on licensure was placed on the books, many small and medium-sized homes were closed up. The pressure to comply with the rigid regulations caused considerable soul-searching on the part of the small operators, and many felt that "the game was not worth the candle," in their words. The larger homes, with larger fees, were clear-cut profit ventures with an extra fee for anything beyond the standard necessities. Bigger boarding homes bring about economies, a technical division of labor, and a more rigid scheduling of activities, including meals, bed time, visiting hours, and the like.

The Missouri investigators conclude by saying that the future of boarding homes in Missouri is not clearly discernible. I believe that if the trend of stringent regulation continues, these useful and benign arrangements will not be able to operate.

RECENT ALTERNATIVE LIVING ARRANGEMENTS

Recent years have seen a number of attempts to devise new family arrangements for the elderly as a means of solving many of their problems of economic security, dependency, and loneliness. Like earlier forms of cooperative living, these new arrangements are predicated on the notion that unrelated adults can live together as a family.

One experiment carried out in Miami, Florida (United Home Care Services, 1977) involved matching people who had a home to share with isolated elderly people who were seeking housing and companionship. However, the matching process proved to be difficult, and the project was disbanded. The major problem was that people offering their homes wanted household chores performed, while the elderly people seeking homes were unable to perform these tasks.

Another example of an alternative family-type arrangement (Institute for Community Studies, nd) was attempted in Kansas City, Missouri, where the organizers planned to use existing housing for group living among older people. This project, called ALA (Alternative to Living Alone), was a shared living arrangement for people over 55 who were not related. However, the project also disbanded because of the unwillingness of people to move into someone else's home. Moreover, in Kansas City, the initiators found that a geographical problem was insurmountable because people wanted to stay in their own local neighborhood or area and did not wish to move to another part of the city.

A third example of a cooperative housing arrangement for people over 50 is just being started by the Back Bay Aging Concerns Committee and the Gray Panthers of Greater Boston. This is a nonprofit neighborhood project in which houses or apartments will be owned or rented, and the residents will share responsibility for housekeeping, cooking, and household management. The goal is to have younger people share in the living arrangements and household tasks, thus reducing the costs for all concerned.

Another alternative is Community Housing for the Elderly (formerly called Intermediate Housing), initiated by the Philadelphia Geriatric Center (Brody, Kleban & Liebowitz, 1975; Brody, 1978; Kleban & Turner-Massey, 1978; Liebowitz, 1978). The goal of Community Housing in Philadelphia is to provide an innovative option for older people who need a new living arrangement. Community Housing consists of nine one-family semidetached homes in a residential neighborhood bordering the Center. The houses were remodeled to contain three private efficiency apartments, including a bed-sitting room, bath, and kitchen, with a shared living room. This enables the residents to maintain independence, privacy, and a normal life-style, but still to have easy access to supplementary services if they need them. Residents can purchase housekeeping service, linen services, and frozen dinners from the Philadelphia Geriatric Center. This program has been very effective from all points of view—satisfaction with housing, improved health status and mortality compared with control groups, and satisfaction with the neighborhood.

In addition, there are two excellent programs set up by Jewish service organizations. The first is the Group Home Program of the Jewish Council for the Aging (a private, nonprofit multiservice agency for senior citizens, supported in part by the United Jewish Appeal Federation of Greater Washington) (Van Dyk & Breslow, 1978). Its principal goal is to help older people stay in the community.

This group realized that some clients were not able to remain in their own residences, despite a battery of supportive services. They have eight three-bedroom apartments serving 24 residents, all of whom have some degree of physical or mild mental impairment.

There is an extensive service arrangement—a social worker directs the program, assisted by a part-time case worker. They visit each apartment at least weekly. There is also a part-time homemaker service, as well as an ongoing recreation schedule, and twice a week the residents are provided mini-bus service to the Jewish Community Center for classes and organized recreation. Activities also are scheduled in the social room in the apartment building on three other weekdays. Charges are set at $415 a month, but this does not meet the costs of the program. Government subsidies and funds from the Jewish Council for the Aging make up the difference. The program is still under evaluation, but it seems to be an important form of sheltered housing for a homogenous subgroup with an umbrella organization providing leadership and guidance.

A similar arrangement reported by Wax (1976) has been developed by the Jewish Federation of Metropolitan Chicago. Although the experiment has some similarities to other alternative forms, there are some differences: It has a strong backup of social services provided by the sponsoring agency, including a resident case worker who is present five days a week, and a psychiatrist who is on call. The program also boasts a rich array of volunteers organized by the social agency. The ecology of the Chicago alternative involves a complex of town houses, rather than a single building as in Washington.

SHARE-A-HOME—A PRAGMATIC AMALGAM*

Share-a-Home, a new and ingenious concept which has proved successful in Florida, is solving the problems of housing and family life for ambulatory elderly people. The concept is a "family" of nonrelated senior adults who share their own household and divide up the expenses of running it. The cost averages from $375 to $425 a month, which is less than half the costs of most nursing homes. This makes it a far less expensive solution for the isolated, slightly dependent older person who cannot live alone.

An Orlando businessman, James Gillies, helped the first family to organize in 1969. This original unit of 20 elderly persons jointly owned a 27-room house and facilities. A salaried

*This section has been adapted from "An Alternative Family Form for Older Persons: Need and Social Context" by the author in *The Family Coordinator,* October, 1978, *27,* 413–420.

manager and staff took care of finances and housekeeping and was responsible for providing food, transportation, laundry service, and the like. The family retained the privilege of keeping or dismissing the management.

Some cooperataive living arrangements specify the sharing of tasks by family members, but Share-A-Home was organized from a different premise. The organizers believed it was unrealistic to expect older people with varying degrees of ability and disability to cooperate harmoniously in preparing food, shopping, planning meals, housekeeping, overseeing special diets, monitoring medication, providing transportation, arranging for medical attention when members are sick, and so on. Therefore paid staff members perform these necessary tasks. The monthly share of expenses covers all household costs including rent, food, maintenance, and staff salaries. Each family owns or leases a car, and the management is responsible for providing transportation to members for medical service to the physician of their choice, or to church, shopping, the hairdresser, club activities, and the like.

No admission fees are charged, no contract is signed, and members may withdraw from the family at any time. To be accepted for membership in a family, an elderly person must be ambulatory, must be able to take care of her or his own person, must have had a recent physical examination, and must have given someone power of attorney. New members have a 30-day trial period before being accepted or withdrawing.

After the first family was successfully established, there appeared to be a need for other units, and others were formed in the Orlando and Winter Park areas. As the number of families grew, there was also a need to set up an association to help form new families, and the Share-A-Home Association, Inc. was founded. This is a nonprofit, tax-exempt organization chartered in 1972 under the laws of the State of Florida. It has a board of 11 directors chosen from the community. While the Association does not manage the families' affairs in an institutional sense, it loans funds to families to get started, to make basic repairs, or to buy furnishings.

A variety of housing has been adapted: One occupies a former Catholic convent, another is in a spacious mansion, another in a six-bedroom ranch house, two are in former Rollins College buildings, and others are in various kinds of dwellings in residential neighborhoods that can accommodate from eight to 20 persons. The utilization of a variety of building structures is indicataive of the overall pragmatism and adaptability of the Share-A-Home idea.

The term *family* has meaning for the residents, for they live together, eat together, work together and play together. Further, they share a number of other things: birthdays, outings, expenses, fun, and joys. They have the security of a home, and they share the feeling that they are part of something worthwhile.

Thus the Share-A-Home families meet three important socio-psychological needs that have been stressed in many studies of aging: (1) free choice, (2) association with others who give affection and concern, and (3) feelings of dignity and autonomy.

To summarize, Share-A-Home is not a traditional family, but it does have many family characteristics and it has been considered a family on some legal grounds (Sussman, 1976). At the same time the organizational structure of the Association (such as having a board of directors) shows formal characteristics typical of a bureaucratic organization. As an *amalgam group* (primary and bureaucrataic), a Share-A-Home family tries to deal with both uniform tasks and nonuniform tasks, and its social structure and function suggest the need for a sharper understanding of how it might provide important services for some older Americans.

The analysis of Share-A-Home as a mixed social structure forming a unique amalgam indicates that it combines the need for trained experts in certain areas—a characteristic of bureaucrataic groups—and also the need for flexibility, sensitivity, and concern in interpersonal relations—a characteristic of primary groups. It is clear that the goals, the recruitment process, the training of personnel, the development and invoking of rules, and the modes and types of reward and punishment are fundamentally different in bureaucratic structures and primary groups. It is this unique amalgam structure that makes Share-A-Home interesting to both theorists and practitioners in the fields of gerontology and family studies.

CONCLUSION

The previous discussion of alternative living arrangements for the elderly indicates that gerontologists, practitioners, and administrators have been active in trying to initiate new forms of living arrangements which lie on the continuum between complete autonomy and complete institutionalization.

In many instances it is too early to offer an analysis on the benefits, costs, and success or failure of these arrangements (Liebowitz, 1978). Some have been operating for only a short time with financial support from model projects and demonstration grants. In the immediate future, we will probably have more research and demonstration projects that will enable us to determine more precisely which models will work and which will not. Obviously, we will need more detailed data about the factors that get these projects started, and those variables that ensure continuity and success.

The transformations of our family structure and social welfare system have resulted in new standards: Matters that were formerly considered private and familial are now matters of public policy, public administration, and public funding. However, at the same time the United States retains a highly individualistic value system, linked to a profit-making economy which assumes a high degree of individual responsibility.

We have described the Florida alternative as a living arrangement for the elderly which meets the needs of the slightly impaired elderly for care, sociability, transportation, and security in a family-like environment at relatively low cost. Residents can exercise a high degree of independence if they wish; however, many supports are offered for those who need them. The idea has spread beyond Florida, and over a hundred letters have been received from individuals and groups asking for more detailed information on how to set up such a family. What are the possibilities of its adoption in other states?

First, there is the problem of housing regulations. Share-A-Home uses existing residences, often gracious old homes in established neighborhoods. Regulations in some states may specify so many requirements that some Share-A-Homes could not meet them. For example, some states give careful specifications for room size, window ratio to floor space, plumbing, stairways, bathrooms, ceiling height, and so on—specifications that only an institution built especially for the purpose could meet. Most older homes would need so much remodeling that the cost would be prohibitive.

Such regulations were drawn up to prevent some of the very distressing conditions existing when helpless people are "warehoused"—especially those discharged from hospitals in large cities. It is true that there have been a few exposés of shocking living conditions when profit-making entrepreneurs have crowded too many people into a small space and kept them virtually prisoners, while receiving large amounts of public funds. However, most people needing sheltered housing are not helpless and they should not be treated as prisoners.

A second problem is staffing. The trend in setting up state regulations is to specify staff positions and determine academic training for each. The type of managers who are most effective and successful in Share-A-Home are often motherly women with great compassion and common sense but no formal credentials.

If alternative living arrangements are to be practical, we must devise ways to establish and operate them at low cost. We must not set up such a rigid system of rules and regulations—always guarding against the rare case of abuse—that we deny the majority the right to a life-style of their choice, or that we force people into institutional settings when they really need only sheltered living conditions.

To be more specific, one way that service delivery systems can enhance their operation is to use volunteers. In the care of the elderly, this has been a major policy recommendation in the last few years. Volunteers provide a needed service and play a meaningful role. Under the regulations of one state, it is specified that each person, including volunteers, must have a TB screening test and the test must be on file. Does this mean that if a Girl Scout troop came in to offer recreational programs and serve refreshments that all the girls would have to have TB tests?

Regulations such as this were placed on the books with good intentions and for a sound purpose. However, when carried out to the letter, such regulations could prevent the founding of alternative living arrangements or discourage volunteers from trying to enrich the program and improve the residents' quality of life.

This leads us to a more basic question: How much risk should society tolerate? The answer is complicated and cannot be addressed in a few sentences. All of us will have to give it further thought, but in my opinion this is another one of those areas in which we find ourselves in a cultural bind. In some areas of life, we are excessively cautious, but in others we are unconcerned about the risks to ourselves and to other Americans. Most people accept risks on our highways with equanimity; there is general indifference to the 55-mile-an-hour speed limit. In fact, there is even scorn on the part of many for this so-called infringement of one's rights, even though the lower speed limit has been proved to save thousands of lives and millions of dollars in property damage.

Some believe that if we write better and more regulations to protect the elderly, we can prevent any accident, mishap, or exploitation. In reality, such a goal is impossible. Moreover, the American public will not pay the necessary taxes to enable all older citizens to live in the conditions specified in the laws. In fact, many of the general public do not live under such conditions.

There have been so-called tax revolts in many states and other moves to limit public expenditures for health and welfare. If rules such as these are eventually adopted in all states, who will pay for the inspection and enforcement required? Or who will pay for the double or triple cost of keeping such elderly in approved institutions, when they could live in a more informal and far less expensive alternative arrangement?

A further problem is the paperwork that is increasingly becomig required. Low-cost family-type living arrangements do not have the additional staff needed to maintain the records required by some states. If one is trying to maintain a family-like living environment, bureaucratic red tape has to be kept to a minimum. The greater the amount of record keeping and the longer the reports that are required, the more institutionalized the home becomes. A considerable amount of record keeping and monitoring of persons is predicated on the reasonable notion that this information will ensure compliance with the law and thereby ensure better service. However, record keeping and report writing are not necessarily correlated with better service delivery and happier elderly people.

In Share-A-Home the emphasis is on personal attention to the resident, and the underlying philosophy is that it is more important for a staff person to talk to a resident, if that is what the resident needs at some particular moment, than to complete a particular household task. A living arrangement that is to function in a family-like manner cannot be formalized by over-rigid rules and regulations.

I have tried to present an overview of the various and diverse living arrangements for the elderly that attempt to provide a satisfactory environment for older persons who are unable to live independently in their own homes or apartments and yet are not sufficiently ill, frail, or dependent to require institutionalization. Some of these alternatives, such as the boarding home, have been utilized to care for the elderly in our society for a long time. Others are more recent developments which involve marshaling private and governmental funds and utilizing both professional and nonprofessional staff.

All of us are concerned with humane, satisfying, and inexpensive solutions for the housing needs of frail older Americans. Four issues, it seems to me, are paramount in trying to reach these objectives.

The first issue related to alternative housing is financing; in short, who pays? The major sources of financial support are the residents themselves, their relatives, charitable persons and organizations, the staff, and government agencies—federal, state, and local. Some of the innovations have been funded by demonstration or model project grants. The question that immediately arises is "What happens when the model project monies are cut off?" In the case of the Share-A-Home alternative and some other cooperative housing arrangements, no governmental subsidy was received. Residents do receive income from social security, of course.

Second, we must consider the size of the living units. If a noninstitutional atmosphere is to be established, we should encourage the formation of alternative living arrangements in which the number of residents is small. This means that at any

one meal there should not be more than 15 people. This suggestion is an intuitive one, for we do not have research on what is the
critical mass for an effective and satisfying living arrangement.

A third issue that we should consider is whether the living
arrangement places the interest of the investors before that of the
residents. In a society that considers profit making a socially
valuable endeavor and in which about 80% of our nursing homes
are proprietary and run for profit, it may seem naive to suggest
the minimizing of profit taking in the area of alternative living
arrangements. However, my brief review of existing alternatives
suggests that it is possible to provide low-cost housing without
exploitation.

This leads me to my last point—that one way to ensure safe,
humane, decent alternative living arrangements is to maximize
their visibility. Many of the alternative arrangements that I have
described are opened to public visits by the sponsors and organizers. Community participation of church and civic groups should
be actively encouraged—not only for its inherent benefits to the
residents, but because visibility ensures safety.

Another possibility is the use of a sponsor system, as it is
employed in the Missouri boarding house arrangement. This
should also increase the visibility of the residents and the conditions under which they live.

The field of alternative living arrangements is just beginning. We will need all the ingenuity and initiative that gerontologists can muster, and flexibility on the part of rule-makers and
administrators, for the need is great and we know that it will
increase considerably in the years ahead.

References

Albrecht, R. Retirement hotels in Florida. In C. C. Osterbind (Ed.),
    Feasible planning for social change in the field of aging. Gainesville:
    University of Florida Press, 1969.
Brody, E. M. Community housing for the elderly: The program, the
    people, the decision-making process, and the research. *The Gerontol-
    ogist,* 1978, *18,* 121–128.

Brody, E. M., Kleban, M. H., & Liebowitz, B. Intermediate housing for the elderly: Satisfaction of those who moved in and those who did not. *The Gerontologist,* 1975, *15,* 350–356.

Bultena, G. L., & Wood, V. The American retirement community: Bane or blessing? *The Journal of Gerontology,* 1969, *24,* 209–217.

Erickson, R., & Eckert, K. The elderly poor in downtown San Diego hotels. *The Gerontologist,* 1977, *17,* 440–446.

Habenstein, R. W., Kieffer, C., & Wang, Y. Boarding home for the elderly: Overview and outlook. Columbia, Missouri: Center for Aging Studies, University of Missouri, 1976.

Hochschild, A. R. *The unexpected community.* Englewood Cliffs, NJ: Prentice-Hall, 1973.

Institute for Community Studies, Kansas City, Missouri. Summary report: Alternate living arrangements. Report to the Administration on Aging, n.d.

Jacobs, J. *Fun city: An ethnographic study of a retirement community.* New York: Holt, 1974.

Kleban, M. H., & Turner-Massey, P. Short-range effects of community housing. *The Gerontologist,* 1978, *18,* 129–132.

Lally, M., Black, E., Thornock, M., & Hawkins, J. D. Older women in single room occupant (SRO) hotels: A Seattle profile. *The Gerontologist,* 1979, *19,* 67–74.

Liebowitz, B. Implications of community housing for planning and policy. *The Gerontologist,* 1978, *18,* 138–143.

Newman, S. J. Housing adjustment of the disabled elderly. *The Gerontologist,* 1976, *16,* 312–317.

Rosow, I. *Social integration of the aged.* New York: The Free Press, 1967.

Stephens, J. *Loners, losers, and lovers: Elderly tenants in a slum hotel.* Seattle: University of Washington Press, 1976.

Sussman, M. B. The family life of old people. In R. H. Binstock & E. Shanas (Eds.), *Handbook of aging and the social sciences.* New York: Van Nostrand Reinhold, 1976.

United Home Care Services. Share-a-home pilot project: Summary, evaluation, findings. Miami, Florida. Report to the Administration on Aging, 1977.

Van Dyk, M. W., & Breslow, R. W. Evaluation of the Jewish Council for the Aging group home program. Rockville, Maryland: Jewish Council for the Aging of Greater Washington, 1978.

Wax, J. It's like your home here. *New York Times Magazine,* Nov. 21, 1976, p. 38ff.

Chapter 5

SRO ELDERLY

A Distinct Population in a Viable Housing Alternative

Phyllis Ehrlich and Ira F. Ehrlich

As more persons live longer with chronic disabling conditions due to mental or physical impairment, society is faced with an urgent need to develop rational and humane policies to maintain such persons with dignity within their own communities. Recognizing the vital role of long-term care institutions, we know they can never begin to meet the housing and service needs of this population. Also, the high cost of this long-term care makes it prohibitive as a model source of housing and services. Therefore, we need community housing alternatives. One of these is single room occupancy (SRO) housing hotels or rooming houses.*

*SRO housing characteristics (prepared by SRO National Executive Board, Senate Information Paper 1978): furnished rooms with or without self-contained bathrooms; usually without kitchens (may be communal); some management services (desks, linens, housekeeping); permanent occupants (at least half the tenants); commercial establishment (neither subsidized nor licensed for institutional care); frequently the facility is old and deteriorated, with electrical or plumbing systems that need replacement; usually these facilities are located in commercial areas.

As mentioned in the Information Paper "Single Room Occupancy: A Need for National Concern" (1978), the number of hotels, the profile of tenants, and the involvement of local government vary from city to city. But one thing is becoming clearer and clearer. SROs are *not* limited to large cities or urban areas. Besides New York City, San Francisco, Los Angeles, St. Louis, Detroit, Chicago, and Philadelphia, SROs are also found in Charleston, West Virginia, Big Stone Gap, Virginia, Sioux City, Iowa, Benton, Illinois, and many other communities.

SRO hotels are not just for the elderly. In fact, normally the elderly do not constitute a majority of their clientele. However, research reports from two recent SRO national conferences and other studies of this population indicate that the elderly population is high where SRO hotels are found. Whereas persons 65 and older constitute 10% of the U.S. population, random surveys across the country indicate that single elderly populations in center cities may range as high as 49%. Bohannon (1976) suggested that the single younger SRO residents tend to assume the characteristics of the SRO elderly.

The last 10 years have seen increased attention given to this population. The plight of the individuals, the ecological changes, and the apparent isolation of this population from traditional community service systems have become issues for a number of researchers across the country. The bias of these action-oriented researchers is that this group should no longer be shunted aside by a community endeavoring to eliminate their needs through destroying their environment. Concern on the part of researchers is far from sufficient to address this situation. The practitioner must become an ally working to remove the SRO elderly population from a position of double jeopardy—old age and an SRO residence—vis-à-vis the problems of aging within a chosen life-style and its relationship to the formal service systems.

The goals of this article are (1) to raise the consciousness of human service workers toward the needs of this distinct elderly population, (2) to provide information based on specific research data about the general population characteristics and environmental support systems, and (3) to propose worker roles appropriate to the needs and value systems of this group.

POPULATION IDENTIFICATION

To increase their awareness of the needs of this specific population, workers should become familiar with the people as individuals. A few vignettes may serve the purpose here.

Arthur Calfyon, 82, a retired barber, was pressured one night to leave his hotel when a new owner decided to evict the long-term residents of the Rutledge Hotel in Manhattan. For 25 years Mr. Calfyon had lived in this hotel in a single room and had never missed a week's rent. The landlord used the tactic of refusing to accept residents' rent payments, claiming they were transients, in order to renovate the old hotel and considerably raise rents. "Where they gonna put me—in a pothole?" Mr. Calfyon asked the nonlistening world as he bent over and moved slowly with a cane. "To go out to the corner cafeteria I have to stop three times. Where they gonna put me? With some junkies somewhere?" (*New York Post*, June 4, 1974).

In Philadelphia the last two guests of Philadelphia's Bellevue Stratford Hotel—a place for the rich, certainly not a place for the poor—moved to another hotel in the downtown area only a few blocks away. They were a 93-year-old and a 64-year-old who had lived in the hotel for over 20 years (Associated Press, November 27, 1976).

Ray lived six years in a St. Louis hotel before it was razed. He lived in a 7' × 8' room on a less than $100 monthly disability check. He lived on food stamps and had a small burner in his room on which he did a lot of his own cooking. He liked to paint, occasionally talked to one or two of the other men, knew most of the men to say "hi" but didn't know them personally. He'd sooner stay up in his room and paint than sit around and talk or argue. He asserted his strong need for privacy and independence by saying "I don't like for people to ask me where I'm going or where I've been" (Case Study, St. Louis, SRO Program).

One generalized poignant description of SRO was developed by Jim Hampton, an editorial reporter of the *National Observer*. He spent a number of days interviewing SRO residents, and in 1976 wrote a feature story which captured their unique life-style:

The invisible elderly are the elderly poor who live alone in single rooms in cheap, usually old and often decrepit urban hotels. These people live their alienated lives in every American city that has such hotels and they're scattered among small town boarding houses as well. Loners by choice, they often spend their entire adult lives downtown. When they move, it's usually from squalid hotel to squalid hotel, just one surge ahead of the redeveloper's wrecking ball. Grown old, without family, friends, funds, or a future, they nonetheless treasure their independence and sometimes shun help when it's offered. One researcher terms their life style "anonymity in proximity". They live close to but apart from other people. They're (usually) uninvolved and hence politically voiceless. They've lived outside the system so long that few know how to tap its benefits even when they'd like. They ask nothing of society but to be left alone, and so to society they're invisible.

St. Louis SRO Elderly Study

This descriptive picture is verified by the findings of a study of the St. Louis SRO elderly population (Ehrlich, 1976). This study sought to describe people 60 years old or older, who lived alone in single rooms of hotels which did not provide any formal supportive services such as meals or recreation programs, and which were located in downtown commercial area.

For the period of data collection, it was estimated that 250 elderly SROs lived in 16 hotels of the downtown area. A canvas of 13 of these hotels (three would not cooperate) identified 111 subjects who agreed to be interviewed. Interviews were conducted in private in the hotel.

The study explored the following areas: personal biography (including socioeconomic position and length of downtown residence); informal support system (including friendships and visiting patterns); formal support systems (including location and use of community resources and services), and self-perceptions of physical and mental health (including daily living patterns, self-disclosure, medications, and priorities of personal concern). In summary the St. Louis study suggests these characteristics:

1. A distinct SRO personality type and life-style built upon an "alone" (from others and systems) pattern of existence;
2. A preference for a downtown or commercial area SRO residence and community to continue this life-style;
3. An undergirding of the continuity of this life-style preference through a strong interrelationship between the residents' personalities and the environmental factors (Figure 5-1);
4. The need to preserve the integrity of this life-style because of its importance as a suitable life style option for some.

More specifically, the SRO elderly respondent in the St. Louis sample saw himself in a "wellness" frame of reference— physically and psychologically. He recounted only a mild history of sickness and, most interestingly, showed few of the stress-related illnesses of the aged in spite of low usage (14%) of community health resources. This could suggest that the SRO population exemplifies the survival of the fittest. This group apparently did not let health problems, identified by a like-aged group of persons, become problems for them; they seemed to disregard typical symptoms and resulting diseases and to survive the disease or conditions by sheer will power.

The psychological profile indicated a population that disclosed very little of itself. They neither told about themselves nor

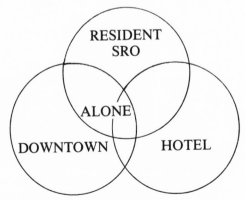

Figure 5-1.   SRO-interrelated living pattern.

allowed themselves to be "bothered" by external environmental infringements such as deteriorating hotels and declining neighborhoods, or by gaps in their personal life-styles through lack of close friends or relatives.

The SRO pattern of "aloneness" was determined by (1) self-disclosure (Jourard & Lasakow, 1958), that is, the process of sharing one's personal thoughts with another, and (2) documented interrelationship patterns among hotel residents. The findings demonstrated that while emotional well-being for this population was not related to self-disclosure, it also was not related to a confidant relationship. (The confidant theory [Lowenthal, 1968] is well-accepted in psychological literature today). Basically, then, one sees a consistent pattern of noninvolvement and noninterrelationship in which there is distance between persons living in close proximity.

It is important to note that even with the above nonconfidant relationship pattern, there is still a superficial informal support system that may operate in times of personal need. One of the few studies that offers some explanation for this informal though weak support network suggests that the SRO norms of utilitarianism, freedom, and privacy govern the types and frequency of social relationships permitted among them (Stephens, 1975). These norms were observed to be operative. Opportunity for forming relationships with tenants on a personal basis was restricted by the respondents. Maintaining privacy went beyond staying out of each other's rooms; it also included not sharing one's personal affairs with others.

Since the St. Louis study was based on a self-selected sample, its findings can only be suggestive of the larger and almost literally invisible population. However, support for the overall concept of an SRO downtown personality is provided by the findings of other studies as well, conducted in diverse areas such as Syracuse, New York (Rubenstein, 1976), Detroit, Michigan (Stephens, 1973), and San Diego, California (Bohannon, 1976). Whether one is talking of new or old residents, male or female residents, young or old residents, or expensive or cheap hotels, the patterned responses hold firm and give credence to a distinct population, though certainly not a homogenous one.

SRO HOUSING HOTEL

If most people living in SROs are those crippled by the double jeopardy of old age and an SRO residence, why are SROs still considered a viable form of housing? Many of the facilities are old and were originally built for transients. The bare light bulb, the chipped paint, the noisy radiators, the chairs with stuffing coming out do not represent housing choices for most; not even most SRO elderly would opt for this if similar but better facilities were available at comparable rents. Rentals frequently remain higher in SRO hotels than they would be for small apartments in other sections of the city. Yet, even though there are fewer choices because of the gradual demolition of hotels, residents tend to stay in the SRO area, moving from one hotel to another. And despite deteriorated systems in constant need of replacement, there are many reasons why SRO hotels may be considered a satisfactory, desirable source of housing for some people. These reasons are paraphrased (and reordered) from those delineated in the *U.S. Senate Information Paper* (1978).

Individual Factors

1. This form of housing is actively chosen by many older persons. In many instances it was their choice years ago when there were a variety of alternatives available at a similar cost.
2. Personal security may be enhanced because people are always on the premises, and a desk clerk or superintendent is usually on duty.
3. Frequently, assumptions of what is right and necessary for people to live comfortably are based on standards that are not those of the people in question. Kitchens and private bathrooms are often not considered necessary by many older people who have never had them. Heat, security, and cleanliness are much more important to the quality of life of tenants than room size or even private bathrooms.
4. SROs frequently are an alternative to institutionaliza-

tion. Substantial savings are realized if SRO tenants can maintain an independent life-style and avoid becoming residents of public nursing or long-term care institutions.

Community Factors

1. Moderate renovation to improve these facilities is far less costly than gut rehabilitation or demolition and new construction. Operating costs and maintenance are approximately the same as in a new building.
2. Relocation of tenants to permit demolition or rehabilitation is very expensive to taxpayers. In addition, it creates major upheaval in the lives of the tenants relocated and almost invariably results in a lowering of their standards of living.
3. SROs most frequently exist in commercial or downtown areas of the city. If a commitment is made to SROs as a viable form of housing, then planning for urban redevelopment can encourage coexistence of SROs and other development.

SRO ELDERLY AND THE SERVICE SYSTEM

The report of the National SRO Executive Committee meeting in St. Louis in 1977 (U.S. Senate Information Paper, 1978) stated that large segments of the SRO population are unable to make proper use of community services on their own. They hypothesized that fear of being institutionalized and lack of trust are two major factors keeping this group of people from using available, needed services. The negative attitudes of many of the service providers in times of crisis compound the problem.

The complexity of the situation vis-à-vis the SRO elderly and the service system is poignantly portrayed by Anne Strozier (1976) in her case study of the "huge sterile bureaucratic hospital and the single, poor, dirty, uncommunicative and unhealthy hotel dweller." At the time of patient admission, neither trust nor understanding could be found in either the health care provider or the patient. Strozier intervened to assist the health care system in dealing positively and appropriately with both the ailments and idiosyncrasies of the SRO elderly patient. She gave the patient the assurance that someone in this large impersonal system cared about him as a human being. Such sensitive, dedicated workers are not always easy to find for the SRO elderly in health care or other services.

Evidence is accumulating that in many states, patients discharged from mental hospitals are increasing the SRO population tremendously because of accelerated programs for "returning people to the community." What we can expect is that this movement has added a new dimension to the life-styles and to the problems of the people who have chosen SROs as places to live. This movement has put a burden on these ex-patients, and on the elderly already residing in SROs. Even though SRO elderly rarely have confidant relationships, they still have had some kind of a mutual support network. The discharged mental patient brings to the SRO problems of extreme loneliness, isolation, and even severe malnutrition.

Proposed Service Delivery System

As discussed above, two major needs of persons without a family and living an SRO life-style are housing and services. In times of crisis the SROs need services related to health, finance, psychological problems, and other basic concerns. However, since these elderly people rarely have a confidant, and since they have been out of the system for so long, they don't know how to enter it. When they do, they find bureaucratic methods alien to their life-styles. Thus they need services delivered in a mode that is consistent with their life-style, which may require a nontraditional, flexible approach on the part of the service providers—not more "business as usual".

To serve both the traditional SRO elderly population and the returned patient, bridges must be built between the workers in the agencies and the clients in the community. In this way what can be offered will be just what this increasingly isolated and alienated SRO population needs. Their lack of trust and concomitant need to get back into the social and medical system can be ameliorated through the training of SRO-oriented outreach workers who may need to spend hours, days, or weeks building relationships to help overcome this fear and distrust of agencies. At the same time these workers will have to build bridges of understanding from the workers in the agencies back to their clients. These responsibilities would expand the accepted outreach worker roles of population identification, needs assessment, and referral. They are responsibilities that also require professional understanding and acceptance of individual autonomy for those whose life-style may be very different from the workers. They are responsibilities that require the ability to move among diverse service settings and housing environments in times of crisis. They are responsibilities that include roles of leadership and support through a generalist social work approach.

Still, conscientious workers implementing such skills could have a negative rather than a positive impact on the environment unless their work is designed within the SRO life-style framework. Every effort must be made not to "formalize" the informal system of this environment, not to make the hotel a community-based institution with standardized, ongoing activities. It is this very unsystemized ad hoc nature of the peer services that make them successful in SROs, and upon which the worker must build.

Even if one is successful in building these bridges and providing these necessary one-to-one services, only the tip of the iceberg will have been touched. Workers who meet only the personal needs of SRO residents, even within the methodology suggested above, would be applying a Band-Aid to a gaping wound. They would be providing services to a population while their housing environment is coming down around them. Thus the issue is much larger than meeting personal needs alone; the issue is becoming an advocate for and, where possible, with this noninvolved, isolated, and perhaps alienated population. This population may choose to live in downtown hotels, but if even simple, adequately maintained rooms are available, they won't choose a poorly lit, inadequately heated or cooled living space.

Thus, as suggested in the statement "SRO Update—A Call to Action" in the *Senate Information Paper* (Ehrlich, 1978), "It is vital that local service deliverers understand that the policy issue here is not only of respect for the preservation of a lifestyle but the preservation of a type of housing as well."

Conclusion

SRO hotels and rooming houses are a widespread and national phenomenon. They allow for some flexibility and choice in life-style for persons with limited economic and social resources. The immediate surroundings encourage support networks to arise, if the residents wish. Irving Rosow (1967) states that this pattern of living allows for insulation but not isolation. The service systems do not recognize the distinct characteristics of this population; they meet neither their day-to-day nor their crisis needs.

> Society turned away from SRO occupants a long time ago, and now they sincerely believe we don't care. These are people who have not been considered or involved in the planning process, thus, they have been moved and dislocated for parking lots, civic centers, and high-rise buildings. They are moved because they are poor, powerless, and considered unattractive. Destruction of their housing has neither answered their needs nor destroyed their lifestyle. It persists and is viable. They have not been eliminated nor should they be—they must be allowed to exist positively. (U.S.–Senate Information Paper, 1978).

Human service workers must recognize that an agency or group that understands an outreach service philosophy in a generalist framework with an advocacy orientation could ensure that this distinct population has the right to live in decent housing that supports this distinctive life-style. They need your help and they need your advocacy, but in *their* way.

References

Bohannon, P. A community of loners. Paper presented at the 2nd National SRO Elderly Conference, St. Louis, Missouri, 1976.

Ehrlich, P. Study of the "invisible elderly": Characteristics and needs of St. Louis downtown SRO elderly. In *The invisible elderly*. National Council on the Aging, 1976.

Ehrlich, P. SRO update—A call to action. *In Single room occupancy: A need for national concern.* An Information Paper prepared for use by the Special Committee on Aging, U.S. Senate, Washington, 1978.

Hampton, J. They're old, alone, poor—They're the invisible elderly. *National Observer,* June 26, 1976.

Jourard, S., & Lasakow, P. Some factors in self-disclosure. *Journal of Abnormal and Social Psychology,* 1958, *56,* 91–98.

Lowenthal, M. Social isolation and mental illness in old age. In B. Neugarten (Ed.), *Middle Age and Aging.* Chicago: University of Chicago Press, 1968.

Rosow, I. *Social integration of the aged.* New York: The Free Press, 1967.

Rubenstein, D., Shuster, K., & Desierro, F. A study of older persons living in inner city SRO hotels and boarding houses—Syracuse, N.Y. and Charleston, W. Va. School of Social Work, Syracuse University, 1976.

Single room occupancy: A need for national concern. An Information Paper prepared for use by the Special Committee on Aging, U.S. Senate, Washington, DC 1978.

Stephens, J. Society of the alone: Freedom, privacy and utilitarianism as dominant norms in the SRO. *Journal of Gerontology,* 1975 *30*(2), 230–235.

Stephens, J. Loners, losers and lovers: A sociological study of the aged tenants of a slum hotel. Unpublished doctoral dissertation, Wayne State University, 1973.

Strozier, A. SRO and the health system: Case study. In *The invisible elderly.* National Council on the Aging, 1976.

Chapter 6

AGING AND BLINDNESS

Dorothy Demby

Although more is being done these days for disabled and hand-icapped persons, a growing number of older people face blind-ness and severe visual impairment and neglect. The situation is shocking and not too often understood.

For one thing, the main causes of blindness are associated with aging, and people are living longer in spite of chronic illness-es and multiple disabilities. In fact, more than 50% of the people in the United States who are registered as blind (that is, legally blind) are over 65. This means of the estimated total of 490,000 legally blind persons, about 250,000 are elderly (National Society for the Prevention of Blindness, 1977).

Who are they? Some recent data on trends (Lowman & Kirchner, 1979) suggest that by the year 2000, 80% of the 1.756 million older Americans with severe vision impairment will be 75 years and over. The current higher proportion of women will continue. The Health Interview Survey (1963-1965) pointed out that "Of 850,000 elderly persons (65+) reported as severely visually impaired, 64.5% were female." The National Center for Health reports that 25,402 persons, most of them women, are in institutions (Goldstein & Josephson, 1971). In either case, "a contributing factor may be the higher prevalence of diabetes among women—one of the leading causes of blindness—especially among nonwhites." Among aging persons with a vision loss there are also some who have suffered only some vision loss, not total blindness. They are usually multiply impaired and poor, and often end up in an institution. Nonwhites run a higher risk of blindness than whites. Many are not reported to be legally blind because, as previously mentioned, they are often lost in another statistic such as "diabetes."

There is also a group called the "hidden blind," isolates who desire no care and avoid contact with agencies serving the blind (Koestler, 1976). In addition, they must cope with a complex of problems common to elderly, such as loss of hearing, taste, balance, and movement. And these are the very sensory mechanisms needed to learn to adjust to a severe visual impairment. This frustrating irony can be expected to bring about emotional problems. The stress of growing older and becoming blind is so great for some individuals that they withdraw in a variety of ways. The problem is compounded, of course, when the older person with a vision loss is coping with other stresses such as prejudice against ethnic minorities and women.

Take the case of Mrs. X, an 80-year-old black in a mental institution who appears to have a serious vision problem. The observer reports that she is always found alone and neglected. In spite of her alertness, records indicate she is psychotic, homeless, and diabetic. Her case history does not mention the vision problem, but does specify a diet for a diabetic. Diabetes, as previously mentioned, is one of the leading causes of blindness. This is a classic case of blindness that goes uncounted and unserved. Mrs. X becomes a diabetes statistic and another of the "hidden blind."

On the positive side, we find some older persons who do cope with stresses, like Mrs. T, a 94-year-old black who lives alone at home. For her, blindness need not be a total handicap, because the ability to cope with blindness is highly individual. However, there is another shocking situation: In her *The Unseen Minority* (1976), Koestler reminds us that that only 9% of the total resources for blind persons are directed to the needs of the elderly. Yet older persons represent the larger proportion of legally blind people in the United States.

It is important to understand that legal blindness is a definition used to determine eligibility for public assistance. A person is considered legally blind if he can see no more at a distance of 20 feet than someone with normal sight can see at a distance of 200 feet.

In the first three decades of this century, a concentration of services to blind children and blind working adults *was* a reality. At that time, most people became blind because of war, disease, or industrial accidents. They did not live to a ripe old age. As Donald Schon (1970) indicates in his analysis of "the blindness system," today's mismatch of services shows that the system has been unresponsive to changes in the age, needs, and capacities of the blind. He charges that "agencies tend to behave as if they believed that the blind need or should have the services which happen to be offered by the agencies rather than that the agencies should modify services in response to changing characteristics of the blind population" (p. 31). Dr. Schon further explains that this pattern of service is based on many agencies' erroneous view that all blind persons are working-age adults and children who are totally blind. Of course, the shift in the blind population to an older age group negates this point of view.

As we come to realize how many persons fit into this picture, it is sad to face still another alarming fact reported by the National Society for the Prevention of Blindness: 50% of blindness is preventable. This statistic becomes more disturbing when we recognize that about 90% of our information is received through sight (Schloss, 1977), underscoring the importance of blindness prevention.

The vision disorders whose incidence most often increases with age are senile macular degeneration, glaucoma, cataracts, and of course diabetes-related blindness. According to a leading ophthamologist, Dr. Colenbranden, these conditions account for 50 to 60% of all visual loss in those over 45 (Colenbrander, 1978). He explained (Colenbrander, 1978) these eye diseases:

Glaucoma.   With early detection and routine eye examinations, glaucoma can be prevented. Glaucoma is an increase in the pressure inside the eye, which damages the retinal cells. Once damaged, they can't be restored. Glaucoma is an insidious disease, and since it affects peripheral vision first may not even be noticed for a long time. When the individual detects the damage, it is already very extensive. Early detection is essential, and then the increased pressure can be controlled with medication, before the damage is done.

Cataracts. There is no way to prevent cataracts, but there is a cure for them by surgically removing the lens and thus restoring normal vision providing no other defects are present. A cataract forms when there is a clouding on the eye lens, thus preventing the lens from forming an adequate image of the outside world.

Senile Macular Degeneration. Cannot be prevented but sometimes progression can be slowed down. This eye disease usually occurs after age 70 or 80, when retina tissues give out. The longer one lives the greater the chances in developing this disorder. Once it occurs it cannot be reversed nor are preventive measures known.

Perhaps an even more serious factor, related more to statistics on the causes and prevention of blindness, is the accepted view that "more people are blinded by definition than by any other cause" (Colenbrander). The World Health Organization found that 65 different definitions of blindness were used in 65 different countries.

There is now an international move to standardize definitions and terminology on vision loss (Colenbrander, nd). Dr. Colenbrander, the prime mover, pointed out in a recent report that there are three levels of vision loss to consider: normal vision, low vision, and blindness (Table 6–1). (*Low vision* refers to those who aren't blind, but who have such limited vision that even everyday tasks are a challenge.) The different ways of looking at visual loss and its impact on the individual are found in such terms as *visual handicap, vision impairment, visual disability,* and *visual disorder.*

Vision impairment is used to describe the impact these visual disorders have on the functioning of the eye or on how well the eye functions with a certain disorder. The factor described is the functional loss that results. For example, with cataracts the haze blurs fine details, in glaucoma side vision is affected, and in macular degeneration central vision suffers.

Visual Disability describes the performance of an individual

Table 6–1. Visual Impairment, Disability, and Handicap

Visual Impairment
Describes: Reduced function of the eye
Such as: Visual acuity   Color vision
            Visual field   Night vision
            Binocular vision—mobility

Visual Disability
Describes: Reduced abilities of an individual
Such as: Reading skills   Daily living skills
            Mobility skills—orientation   Vocational skills

Visual Handicap
Describes: Need for extra effort; Reduced independence
Such as: Physical independence   Employment
            Mobility   Social integration
            Economic independence

Source: Colenbrander, 1978.

with a vision loss. It is measured in terms of personal skills—reading, orientation, and mobility—and daily living. For example, a person with glaucoma and tunnel vision can see a traffic signal, but not the cars around him; a person with macular degeneration and a central blind spot cannot see the traffic signal, but can see the cars around him. These are visual disabilities affecting an individual's performance.

Visual handicap refers to what an individual can do and is expected to do by friends, family, and associates.Understanding the difference in these terms underscores the need for joint responsibilities in serving older people with vision losses.

- The ophthalmologist, a physician specializing in diseases of the eye, combats visual disorders and impairments.
- Optometrists prescribe optical and nonoptical aids to reduce visual impairment and disabilities. (Opthalmologists also prescribe.)
- Social workers, psychologists, nurses, and rehabilitation workers augment these services with instruction, training, education, counseling, and advocacy.

Thus an interdisciplinary approach is essential in meeting the needs of older visually handicapped persons.

SERVICE NEEDS

What are these needs? What special services do professionals think blind persons should receive? What do blind persons themselves say they need? Although the involved agencies are concerned, existing services for older blind and severely visually impaired people are by no means adequate in quality or quantity.

What is needed are programs, services, and attitudes in institutions and in communities that lead each older visually impaired person to his or her maximum functional independence. This means programs, services, and attitudes that not only assist the older blind person with mobility, communication skills, and orientation to surroundings in or out of an institution, but also with the kinds of programs, services, and attitudes that will help the older person with a vision loss to cope with his own problems and needs as a human being. For example, such services might include a means to keep in touch with the rest of the world through the new Radio Information Service or Talking Books, the means to get where he or she wants to go, special aids for personal care, enough money through benefits such as SSI to have a voice in deciding his or her fate. In other words, these programs should provide the older visually impaired person with the same freedom of choice that any other human being has—a choice, an opportunity, and recognition.

GOALS AND OBJECTIVES

The service goals that should concern any individual, group, agency, or institution wishing to do something about the needs of the older population's sight difficulties include:

- Providing and maintaining of quality services that are accessible, available, adequate, and acceptable to the person with a vision loss.
- Reducing loneliness among those who are old and blind.
- Providing opportunities for service in the mainstream of community life.
- Widening the network of services provided for the aging to include the person with a vision loss.

- Increasing public understanding of the blind person, his potential, and his needs.
- Creating independent living centers for older blind persons, to help them in adjusting to their blindness by assisting with daily living skills, personal care, mobility, and orientation.
- Developing comprehensive health care programs and services including vision care to meet the changing vision needs as people grow older.

Personal goals for an older person with a severe vision loss should be aimed toward:

- An independent life according to maximum capabilities as opposed to a life of total dependency.
- Continuing interest in the world and the people around him or her.
- Participation in a useful or interesting activity toward development of unique inner resources.

NATIONAL EFFORTS

To focus nationwide attention on the problems and needs and goals of older blind persons, the American Foundation for the Blind made a commitment 10 years ago to be a national advocate for programs and services that would lead toward the personal and economic independence of older people with sight difficulties, whether or not they were living in an institution.

The Foundation assumed its advocacy role over the years in a variety of ways: with basic planning, analyses of research, formation of a National Task Force on Geriatric Blindness, formation of a board Advisory Committee on Aging, and two National Conferences on Aging and Blindness as springboards for planning and program development. Specific and related national activities aimed at having a more direct impact on services to older people include:

- The development of a National Policy Statement on Aging and Severe Visual Impairment underscore the uniqueness of each person and his or her capabilities and need for independence.
- Session on blindness at the White House Conference on Aging

and Blindness in 1971 and 1981 to identify issues and recommendations and to prepare background papers.

- Pilot projects in New York, Albuquerque, and St. Petersburg to integrate services for older visually impaired persons in community programs and in retirement communities.
- Outreach projects in rural Chehalis, Washington, and Independence, Missouri, to provide services to home-bound, visually impaired older people.

There were follow-up activities for each of these latter two projects: Vision Screening Fiesta in Albuquerque, and a public education prevention program, "Eye Tips," in St. Petersburg. In Independence, Missouri, for example, the Human Resources Corporation received money from American Foundation for the Blind, identified the service needs of the blind elderly in their city, conducted workshops to bring the blind and the service agencies together, and published a resource book in large print. The local community now has an integrated ongoing service that enables older people to live at home rather than in an institution. (This project, by the way, was an outgrowth of Project Independence—National Voluntary Organization for Independent Living for the Aging.)

- Development of training guidelines, information, and publications, including a fact sheet on aging, and legislative activities.
- National and regional conferences on aging and blindness.
- Statistical data and consultative services for other surveys (for example, a national Episcopal Church Survey).

The Foundation's current thrust in national program development has as its ultimate goal a continuum of social services at the local level to meet the range of changing needs of the older blind person. Although the Foundation has had some success in its advocacy efforts to date, unresolved, unanswered, and unmet needs, and mounting issues continue to affect the lives of older people with a vision loss. Major issues, problems, and gaps include shortcomings in legislation, exchange of information, advocacy, prevention of blindness, continuity of services, an organized body of knowledge, and, not the least, opportunities, options, and choices for the older blind consumer.

The following are some of the more immediate issues on

aging and blindness that were considered in preparing for the
1981 White House Conference on Aging.

1. *Alternative forms of care.* Research and demonstration
   show that it is far less costly to the service provider to
   meet the needs of an older person in his own home,
   rather than in an institution. There are a few models of
   keeping older blind persons at home, but they need to
   be expanded to assess their viability in a variety of
   settings and age ranges. I shall discuss one such program in Virginia later.

2. *Day care centers and home health programs* are increasing
   as a result of interest in options to institutional care.
   Usually those eligible would be unable to travel alone,
   so transportation becomes a major service. Special
   adaptations in the program would be necessary when
   serving the older person with a severe vision loss.

3. *Continuum of care concept.* The changing eye conditions
   of an older person as he moves toward the end of his
   life call for a sequence or continuum of services to meet
   each individual's changing needs. Studies show that
   even where there are aging services to meet changing
   needs
   - of 100 applicants, 60 are turned away;
   - of the remaining 40, only 17 are served;
   - only one of five keep their appointments
     (Martinez, 1978).

   Florida and Montana have some pilot programs, but
   one of the more widely known is in Pima County,
   Arizona. This comprehensive county health program
   includes home, outpatient, and institutional care. It is
   this kind of service that seems applicable to the special
   and changing needs of older blind persons.

4. *Interagency collaboration (networks and working agree-
   ments).* The major problem for the older blind person is
   the problem of *any* aging person: No single agency can
   meet all of the individual's needs. Therefore it is essential to work cooperatively through existing aging programs. It has been found that an exchange of information plus the joint efforts of agencies serving the blind

and agencies serving the aging result in more realistic service to the visually handicapped person.

5. *Consumer-oriented programs (advocacy, self-help, ombudsmen)*. States are becoming more sensitized to the needs of older persons and their power as voters. Michigan, Minnesota, New York, Wisconsin, and Florida are examples. In one state less than 40% of all eligible voters cast a ballot. But 95% of its older population votes. As this voting power grows, more age-oriented legislation will appear on the books. Older blind persons need to become a part of this kind of power to assure meaningful services to meet their special needs. The question is, Are they prepared? And is there legislative support?

6. *Legislative developments*. More than 600 bills affecting older people were introduced by the Carter Administration. Did they resolve the legislative problems affecting older people with a vision loss? No. Why? First, because federal legislation such as Medicare does not cover vision care. The need of most older people to regain useful sight could be corrected by low vision services including eye exams and by prescribed aids like lenses. But these services are costly. In some states such as New York, Medicaid covers lenses and other aids. One agency in New York has an arrangement to get reimbursements under Medicare for eye exams but not for aids.

Amendments to the Rehabilitation Act 1973 now contain an "independent living component" that may cover daily activities, services, and programs for older blind people. It is anticipated that grants will be made to states for these rehabilitation services. The amendments also underscore the importance of advocacy by providing for client assistance projects protecting the rights of clients. However, the 504 amendment of the Act on nondiscrimination on the basis of a handicap may present new legal problems to agencies not prepared to serve the blind.

For the first time, the amendments to OAA mandate that state and area agencies act as advocates in the interest of older people, including the blind. The Com-

prehensive Employment and Training Act (CETA)
Amendment has a new training project to serve older
handicapped by providing supportive services, training, and employment geared to their needs. But more
government funding is needed for special aging projects for the blind. Potential sources are OAA Title 3
and Title 4, (staff training), SSA Title XX, SSI, and
now one hopes, the Rehabilitation Act Amendment.

Resulting Local Programs

One of the most heartening moments for me, as someone
involved in national program development on aging and blindness, comes when I reflect on what others are now doing about
aging and blindness as a result of the Foundation's advocacy
efforts over the past 10 years. Wide interest in the problems of
aging and blindness is evident all over the country. Programs are
being developed which reduce isolation, expand the communication network, increase public understanding provide independent living opportunities, or provide comprehensive eye health
care (prevention and treatment).

One of the most devastating results of vision loss among the
elderly is isolation. One community in Cleveland has established a
peer help program using older persons with vision problems to
provide free daily telephone reassurance to other visually handicapped persons. Coordinated by a 75-year-old volunteer, the
program is sponsored by the Mayor's Commission on Aging. This
program points out the possibilities of directly involving the blind
older person in resolving some of his or her own problems of
loneliness, even though homebound.

One of the more exciting possibilities of widening avenues of
communication for older blind persons is the previously mentioned Radio Information Services. This recent technological
development uses open or closed circuit radio channels to broad-
cast the contents of newspapers, magazines, and books to blind
and other physically handicapped audiences. It has infinite
advantages in helping the homebound older person keep in
touch with daily news, especially shopping bargains and
announcements of new legislation and services. About 47 such
services have now been established in 30 states. And another 17

states are planning to do so. Assessments to date confirm its usefulness in enabling visually handicapped people to live more independent lives.

Another development (Morris, 1978) that should enhance the independence of the older blind person is a vocally indexed recorded dictionary for the visually handicapped. Pronouncing the entry word triggers a cassette to play back the definition. This American Printing House project holds the promise of vocal indexing in other kinds of publications. Mature people are able to use the recorded dictionary with no difficulty. The National Council on the Aging and a California telephone company have been working on a telephone book that can be used by persons with vision loss. So far they have decided on the print size, format, and content of the book.

A demonstration project in San Francisco showed how older blind persons can take an active role in getting others involved in distributing information about services. These blind individuals had first completed an adjustment program that helped them regain their self-esteem and independence. Also in San Francisco a group of agencies cooperated in disseminating information on poor vision to a large audience. Agency staff members were able to deepen their knowledge on working with older persons with vision loss.

Perhaps the single most important issue concerning all older blind persons is unnecessary institutionalization. Blindness is the reason that many elderly people are placed in nursing homes.

In a recent HEW analysis of programs for the disabled (Martinez, 1978), the following gaps were pointed out:

1. Home-based services are too scarce. Most federal financial programs tend to move people out of homes, away from families, and into institutions.
2. There are not enough community facilities often because of inappropriate federal regulations or standards and poor interagency collaboration.
3. There is almost no financial support for programs that help people cope with the crises that result from growing older.

However, the Rehabilitation Services Administration has funded a pilot project in nine states which has successfully proved the cost-benefit value of providing home services as an alternative to institutionalization. In this project the Virginia State Commission for the Blind was the first to make substantial savings by providing services in the client's home.

In another independent living program in Tampa, Florida, over 200 older blind clients are trained in communication skills, problem solving, and assertiveness. This program offers incentives to advance and to participate as an advisor or trainer. A similar outreach program is set up for those who live outside the city limits. About 80% of the trainees make the adjustment toward independence. This program holds special interest because it is an interagency effort.

The program that has had the greatest impact on services for older blind persons is perhaps a laboratory residential rehabilitation center, the Center for Independent Living, in New York City. Serving people over 55, this program emphasizes an effective rehabilitation program aimed at self-determination and self-help. The older blind students are intensely involved in establishing individual goals, and they are assisted by a return to the community. Their rehabilitation often ends in their helping other visually handicapped persons.

The importance placed on keeping older persons in their own homes rather than in institutions does not negate the need for nursing homes for some individuals. One such institution that does provide a means for its older clients to retain maximum independence while in an institution is an experiment in independent living model attached to a nursing home in Decatur, Georgia.

Sheltered Flats, as it is known, consists of a single living-dining-kitchen area, a sleeping area, and a bathing area with an emergency call system for each person. The sleeping area is designed to offer comfort for sleeping only. None of the services are mandatory, nor are they included in the rent. Included in the rent are all utilities except the telephone, and an activities program in a small community center contiguous to the Sheltered Flats property. Meal service is available on request only at the nursing home. For a small charge, the nursing home will transport residents of Sheltered Flats to the nursing home if they wish to have meals there.

What this program confirms is that creative planning can result in new solutions to old problems.

To highlight the little recognized problem of an older blind person I want to mention a program model in continuing education, the first such training program for older blind adults in United States, is affiliated with a community college in Orlando, Florida.

One of the elderly's gravest needs is a comprehensive eye care program that includes prevention as well as treatment of vision problems. A large number of older people do not use these services because they cost too much and Medicare does not cover these costs. This lack of low-vision services robs nearly all legally blind of their dignity and independence. Medicare could cover professional services, vision aids, and consultation. If such a bill were passed, at least 400,000 would benefit. Equally important is the finding that 40% of older people who come for a vision-related service need additional help because of other physical complications.

Among the goals for older blind persons that have not been realized is the establishment of comprehensive health care services to meet the compounded and changing conditions of people as they grow older. As I mentioned, there is such a program in Pima County, Arizona, where blind persons are among those who benefit. During a recent Senate hearing on vision care (U.S. Senate, 1978) one study presented mentioned that there are only an estimated 200 low-vision clinics in the United States; one-third are open half a day; 20% are open one day a week, and 8% are open only 1 1/4 to 2 days.

Most eye problems of older persons could be met in a low-vision clinic through an ophthalmological examination and an examination for low vision aids by an optometrist. At the same time the person could be trained on how to use the lens or device. The main problem is the cost. Until there is adequate legislation on eye care, low vision is not covered. The ideal to work toward is a National Health Insurance as a comprehensive health plan for all Americans.

RESPONSIBILITY

Where does the responsibility lie for developing more of these kinds of programs? It is clear that quality programs can come about only when
- blindness and aging becomes everybody's business
- the burden rests on the sighted along with those who have a sight difficulty.

1. Providers of service (public and private) to the aging population have a responsibility to include the older blind person in their services. States must assume a responsibility to include specific funding and services for this special population in state social service plans and other sources of funding.
2. Area agencies on aging have the responsibility to serve as the local outreach in identifying the needs of the multiply impaired, including persons with a vision loss.
3. Universities have the responsibility to include appropriate curriculum in their centers of gerontology, social work, medicine, psychology, and other areas.
4. Professionals in the areas of gerontology, medicine, and psychology, as well as others such as sociology and economics, have the responsibility to assist in the necessary research and documentation.
5. The blind and visually impaired have the right and the responsibility to speak up to make their needs known.
6. Specialized agencies for the blind in your community have the responsibility to help the visually impaired do this; they have the responsibility to serve as a resource for information, referral, and training on vision impairment for other agencies and institutions. Their work should support better public understanding of vision loss, greater professional insight, more services for the blind in the mainstream of services for the elderly, and greater involvement by the blind and visually impaired themselves with special outreach to the high proportion of blind who are members of an ethnic minority group.

GUIDELINES FOR ACTION

To fill the gaps and provide a continuum of services to meet the expressed needs of older blind persons at the local level, I earlier recommended broad goals and objectives. By way of review, these goals are (1) ensuring mainstream and independent living for the blind individual; (2) providing quality services; (3) reducing isolation; (4) widening the communication network; (5) increasing public understanding; and (6) establishing comprehensive health and vision care programs.

All programs also should take into account the individual differences of the older blind population, the degree of blindness, and the need for routine examinations among all elderly. Training staff and volunteers who work with the aged should be oriented to the special needs, physical and social problems, and individual responsibilities of persons with sight difficulties.

RESEARCH

More research is needed, not only to establish the numbers, but also to define the characteristics and psychosocial factors of the older blind and visually impaired person. More needs to be known about the compensations required for sensory losses due to age, and compounded by blindness. Dr. Eric Josephson, who conducted a study on the characteristics of older people, puts in a plea for a study of the many who are visually impaired, but not labeled blind, and for a study of the adjustments that must be made by the blind person and his or her family. Much more needs to be known of the effect of family attitudes as one copes with the stress of old age and blindness. More program patterns for service are needed to meet the problems of this special older group.

PROGRAMS AND SERVICES

Designs for programs and services at any level need to be concerned with mobility, independence, and the communication problems of the older person with vision impairment. The designs should reflect an integrated network of comprehensive services for blind persons who are, most likely, multiply handicapped. Financial assistance, housework services, companionship, transportation, and communication aids are basic.

Radio information services for the blind, now a developing system for providing information to the blind, opens new avenues of communication to them. Alternate forms of home and community care and freedom of choice are of current concern to the American Foundation for the Blind. The trend is a shift away from institutionalization. Consumer involvement with options in the kind of care is the idea.

FUNDING

Creative use of available local and state funds, including grants in the areas of aging, rehabilitation education, and social services is encouraged and a necessity.

STRATEGY

How often have we found that changes in the field of aging have been so rapid that solutions were often outdated before fully carried out? My final recommendation, therefore, is that to keep pace as planners, it's going to take all possible resources—with interagency cooperation and coalitions on all levels. We in the blindness system and in the aging system also need to make fuller use of the concept of the consumer's right to choose what services are needed and wanted, and under what conditions. Only in this way can services for the older visually impaired person, along with others who are aging, be meaningful.

REFERENCES

Colenbrander, August, M.D. *How Blind is Blind?* Testimony to the U.S. Senate Special Committee on Aging Hearing, August 3, 1978. Washington, DC: U.S. Government Printing Office, 1979.

Colenbrander, August, M.D. *Proceedings Second National Conference on Aging and Blindness. March 1978.* Atlanta, GA.: American Foundation for the Blind.

Colenbrander, August, M.D. *WHO Committee on International Nomenclature for Ophthalmology.* Unpublished document, nd.

Goldstein, Hyman, Ph.D. and Josephson, Eric, Ph.D. The social demography of vision impairment. *U.S. Public Health Review,* 1975, IV, 1.

Koestler, Frances A. *The Unseen Minority.* New York: David McKay, 1976.

Lowman, Cherry, M.Phil. and Kirchner, Corinne, M.Phil. Statistical Briefs National Center for Health Statistics health interview survey prevalence rates. *Journal of Visual Impairment & Blindness,* 1979, 73, pp. 69–73.

Martinez, Arabella. Proceedings of the Second National Conference on Aging and Blindness. Atlanta, GA, 1978: American Foundation for the Blind.

Morris, June. Proceedings Second National Conference on Aging and Blindness. Louisville, Kentucky: American Printing House, 1978.

National Center for Health Statistics. Prevalence of selected impairments in U.S. Washington, DC: U.S. Department of Health, Education, and Welfare, 1963–1965.

National Society for the Prevention of Blindness. New York: NSPB, 1977, Unpublished data.

Schloss, Irvin P. Impact of federal legislation on older blind and severely visually impaired persons. In Rehabilitation of the Older Blind Person: a Shared Responsibility. Switzer Seminar Report. Washington, DC, 1977.

Schon, Donald A. The Blindness System. *Public Interest,* 1970, 18, p. 31.

U.S. Senate Special Committee on Aging. Hearing on Vision Impairment among Older Americans, August 3, 1978. Washington, D.C.: U.S. Government Printing Office, 1979.

Chapter 7

THE RIGHT TO DEATH

Antony G. N. Flew

AN AMERICAN RIGHT TO LIFE

With his usual shrewd grasp of fundamentals, the lawyer Abraham Lincoln once wrote about the Declaration of Independence:

> The authors of that notable instrument . . . did not intend to declare all men equal in all respects. They did not mean to say that all men were equal in colour, size, intellect, moral developments, or social capacity. They defined with tolerable distinctness in what respects they did consider all men created equal—equal in certain "unalienable rights, among which are life, liberty, and the pursuit of happiness." (1857)

It is tempting to digress to support and to labor the point that neither Lincoln nor the founding fathers believed: either that "at birth human infants, regardless of heredity, are as equal as Fords" (Hayek, Note 1) or that some such repudiation of genetic fact is implied or presupposed by any insistence upon an equality of fundamental human rights. But our present concern is with the actual prescriptive and proscriptive content of these particular norms. For us the crux is that they are all, in M. P. Golding's terminology, option as opposed to welfare rights: the former forbid interference, within the spheres described, entitling everyone to act or not to act as they see fit; whereas the latter entitles everyone to be supplied with some good, but by whom and at whose expense is not normally specified (Bandman, Note 2).

Hence, with that "peculiar felicity of expression" which led to his being given the drafting job, Thomas Jefferson spoke not of rights to health, education and welfare—and whatever else might be thought necessary to the achievement of happiness—but of rights to life, liberty, and the pursuit of happiness. It is up to you whether you do in fact pursue (and up to the gods whether you capture) your prey. An option right is thus a right to be allowed, without interference, to do your own thing. A welfare right is a right to be supplied by others with something that is thought to be, and perhaps is, good for you—whether or not you actually want it.

To show that the founding fathers were indeed thinking of option rather than welfare rights, it should be sufficient to cite a passage from Blackstone (1825), which has the further merit of indicating upon what general feature of our peculiarly human nature such fundamental rights must be grounded: from their first publication in 1765, his *Commentaries on the Laws of England* had a profound influence on all the Common Law jurisdictions in North America, an influence that continued well into the Federal period. Blackstone wrote:

> The absolute rights of man, considered as a free agent, endowed with discernment to know good from evil, and with the power of choosing those measures which appear to him to be most desirable, are usually summed up in one general appellation, and denominated the natural liberty of mankind.... The rights themselves ... will appear from what has been premised, to be no other, than that *residuum* of natural liberty, which is not required by the laws of society to be sacrificed to the public convenience; or else those civil privileges, which society has engaged to provide in lieu of the natural liberties to be given up by individuals. (pp. 125–128)

But if those self-evident fundamental, and universal rights are thus option rights, and they surely are, then the right to life must be at the same time and by the same token, the right to death. The interference forbidden must be the killing of anyone against that person's will, and that person's entitlement to choose whether to go on living as long as nature permits.

In saying this I am not, of course, so rash as to maintain that it is something that all or any of the Declaration signers saw and intended. Rather, the claim is, that, irrespective of what they or anyone else appreciated in 1776, this does necessarily follow from what they did then so solemnly declare. It is today even more obvious that, if all men are endowed with certain natural and inalienable rights, then all must include all—black and white together. Yet this now so manifest consequence seems for many years to have escaped many people, up to and including justices of the Supreme Court. So a widespread failure to appreciate what may now appear an obvious implication is not enough to show that it is not really an implication at all.

OPTION RIGHT OR WELFARE RIGHT?

In the lower court decision in the now famous case of Karen Ann Quinlan, Judge Muir denied the plaintiff's request to have the life-sustaining apparatus switched off, indicating that he did not find grounds for any right to die in the Constitution. Insofar as the Declaration is not part of the Constitution, we might concede the point. Yet, in my very unlegal opinion, if the Amendment on which *Roe v. Wade* (1973) was decided really does warrant what the Supreme Court decided that it warranted, then it must surely warrant both suicide and assisted suicide. For in abortion, what the pregnant woman is killing, or getting her doctor to kill for her, is arguably another person with his or her right to life (although this is not an argument that I myself accept). So, if it would be a constitutionally unacceptable invasion of privacy to prevent a woman from killing a fetus or getting someone else to kill it for her, then surely it must be a far more unacceptable incursion to prevent women, or for that matter, men, from either killing themselves or getting someone else to kill them. For in all those secular systems of law in which suicide is still a crime, it is a much less serious crime than murder.

Judge Muir next went on to say that if he were to grant the request of the plaintiff, then "such authorization would be homicide and a violation of the right to life" (Muir, 1975). Since it was not disputed that Karen Quinlan had on at least three occasions insisted that, should this sort of situation arise, she would not wish to be maintained in the condition in which she then was—and still is—Judge Muir's "right to life" becomes one that is at the same time a legal duty. Just that, or substantially that, does seem to be the present position in all those jurisdictions that recognize a right to life. For even where, as in my own country today, suicide itself is not a crime, to assist it still is. At the same time, with very few exceptions, doctors and others are legally required to employ every available means to prolong human life of any kind.

For good measure consider two further statements, one from each side of the Atlantic. The first was made by James Loucks, president of the Crozer Chester Medical Center of Chester, Pennsylvania. He had got a court order to permit his hospital to force a blood transfusion on a Jehovah's Witness who had previously requested in writing that, out of respect for her religious convictions, the hospital do no such thing. Mr. Loucks explained that he and his staff overrode her wishes "out of respect for her rights" (*General Practitioner,* Note 3). The second statement was made by the chairman of a group calling itself the Human Rights Society, set up in 1969 to oppose the legalization of voluntary euthanasia. He said: "There are really no such things as rights. You are not entitled to anything in this universe. The function of the Human Rights Society is to tell men their duties."

It has sometimes been suggested that it is contradictory to speak of a right where the exercise of that putative right is compulsory (Bandman, Note 4). This is certainly a tempting suggestion, and it may be what led the chairman of the Human Rights Society thus categorically to deny what his society pretends to defend. But, if we are going to allow welfare as well as option rights, then this contradiction seems to rise only with the latter.

If that is correct then we can pass, for instance, Article 26 of the 1948 United Nations Universal Declaration of Human

Rights: "Everyone has the right to education. . . . Elementary education shall be compulsory." Yet it will still allow us to reject the combination of a right to join a labor union with any corresponding compulsion so to do. For if the exercise of a welfare right is to be made compulsory, then the justification of the compulsion can only be the good, the welfare, of the persons so compelled. Yet in England at any rate, the spokesmen for the labor unions, and their political creatures in the Labour Party, try to justify forced recruitment on the grounds not (paternalistically) that membership is in the best interests even of those who fail to see this themselves, but (indignantly) on the grounds that all holdouts are freeloaders enjoying the benefits, which it is alleged that the union has brought, without undertaking the burdens of membership.

So, allowing that it can be coherent to speak of a right that its bearers are to be forced to exercise, could there be such a compulsory welfare right to life? The crux here is whether the prolongation of life which this right is proposed to impose can plausibly be represented as being good for the actual recipients of this alleged benefit. But perhaps, before tackling that question, it needs to be said that any answer will leave open the different issues raised by considering the good of others. Certainly, while insisting on a universal human option right to life, in the sense explained above, and while urging always that legal recognition and protection of this right is long overdue, I am myself ever ready to maintain that proper considerations of the good of others makes some suicides morally imperative and others morally illicit. The suicide of Wilson, to better the chances of the remaining members of Scott's last expedition, provides an example of the first type, and an example of the other is the suicide of the American poet Sylvia Plath, effected in another room of the house in which she was living with her young and dependent children.

So long as we confine our attentions to what may vaguely but understandably be called normal times, and to the suicides and suicide attempts of the tolerably fit and not old, it is reasonable enough to hold that in general the frustration of such attempts does further the good of the attemptors. Indeed, any realistic discussion in this area has to recognize that a great many apparent attempted suicides are in truth only dramatized appeals for help, and that many of those genuine attemptors whose attempts are aborted by medical or other interference survive to feel grateful to the interferers. But when we turn to the old, faced perhaps with the prospect of protracted senility, of helpless bedridden incontinence, of lives that will be nothing but a burden both to the liver and to everyone else, then the story is totally different. Here you do have to be some sort of infatuated doctrinaire to maintain an inflexible insistence that all life, any life, is good for the liver.

I will not now repeat more than a word or two of what was said a few years ago with such force and charm by the splendid Doris Portwood (1978) in her book *Common-sense Suicide.* It should be enough to report that as a woman over 65 she sees herself as making, and encouraging her peers to join with her in making, a distinctive contribution to the women's movement. "How many of us," she asks those peers, "attending a friend or relative in her final days (or weeks, or months, or years) have said, 'It won't happen to me. I'll take care of that.' But did we say it aloud? It is time to say it loud and clear. And often." It is time, she concludes, mischievously mimicking the jargon of her juniors, to "declare our intention to start a meaningful dialogue on common-sense suicide" (p. 10).

What I will quote instead comes from a newspaper letter. This letter was written by Margaret Murray, a still very active and much valued member of our Voluntary Euthanasia Society. Two years ago she published an article "declaring my intention to end my own life when increasing helplessness from multiple sclerosis makes it a hopeless, useless burden." (*The Guardian,* 1974). This led to the production of a memorable television program. The present letter was a response to the statement by the Medical Director of St. Christopher's Hospice that "requests to end life are nearly always requests to end pain." That medical director had in that program asserted "that though I might be helpless and actually fed and washed and have other sordid details attended to, my life had a value and I still had something to give." Dismissing this particular piece of sanctimonious self-deception with the question, "Who are these greedy takers?" Mrs. Murray proceeded to deploy three cases:

An eighty-year old army colonel, who realised he was becoming senile, flung himself in front of an Inter-City express as it went through the village where I live. A few months later a Newbury coroner gave a verdict of "rational suicide" on a retired water bailiff who took his own life because increasing infirmities meant it was no longer worth while to him.

And what of sufferers from Huntington's Chorea, never still a moment and unable to speak clearly enough to be intelligible? One of these unfortunates who is well known to me has tried three times to end her own life. (*The Guardian*, 1979).

I have just dealt with the question whether there could be a right to life, the exercise of which is not left to the individual. Such a right, of course, could only be a welfare right, not an option right. The next issue now, is whether the option right to life, as explained above, covertly contains an incongruous and unacceptable welfare element. The suggestion is that a right to life that is at the same time and by the same token a right to anticipate the death that would otherwise have occurred later, must impose on some other person or persons a corresponding duty to bring about that earlier death:

A person's right to be killed gives rise to someone's (or everyone's) duty toward that person. If anyone can be said to have a right to be killed, someone else must have a duty to cooperate in the killing. . . . The important thing is that someone—a doctor, a nurse, a candystriper, a relative intervene actively or passively to end the right-holder's life (Bandman, E. L., and Bandman, B., 1978, p. 141).

This passage is, on the one hand, entirely sound insofar as it insists that all rights must impose corresponding duties. However, since all duties do not give rise to corresponding rights, the converse is false. This logical truth constitutes the best reason for saying that welfare rights do not belong in a Universal Declaration of Human Rights. For who are the people who have at all times and in all places been both able and obligated to provide for everyone: "social security" (Article 22), "periodic holidays with pay" (Article 24), "a standard of living . . . including . . . necessary social services, and the right to security in the event of unemployment, sickness, disability, widowhood, old age or other lack of livelihood in circumstances beyond his control" (Article 25 (1)), to say nothing of the provision that that compulsory elementary education aforementioned "shall further the activities of the United Nations for the maintenance of peace" (Article 26 (2)) [Note 5].

But the same passage is, on the other hand, entirely wrong insofar as it tries to draw out the implications of an option right to life. Such rights do necessarily and as such impose corresponding obligations. These obligations rest uniformly and indiscriminately upon everyone else, not just upon some unspecified and unspecifiable subclass of providers, who may or may not in fact be available and able to provide. But these obligations are obligations not to provision but to noninterference.

In a jurisdiction, therefore, that recognized and sanctioned the option right to life, the people who decided that they wanted to suicide (Note 6) would, if they needed assistance, have to find it where they could. Their legal right to noninterference imposes no legal duty on anyone else to take positive steps to assist, although, of course, this is quite consistent with someone's being under a moral obligation to do so. Here, as always, we have to distinguish questions about what the laws do or should permit or prohibit from questions about what people are morally obliged to do or not to do.

Doctors and the Right to Die

When I first joined the Voluntary Euthanasia Society a quarter of a century or more ago, the emphasis was on extremes of physical pain. The main objective was to get a Voluntary Euthanasia Act, which would establish official machinery to implement the wishes of those terminal patients who urgently and consistently asked for swift release. In response to medical and other developments in the intervening years, the emphasis has shifted. It is now on irreversible decay into helpless futility, and on operations resulting in prolonged but not especially painful survival at a subhuman level. The chief and most immediate objectives are also different. The Young Turks, at any rate, as well as their more wide-awake and forward-looking seniors, are now pushing for amendment of the Suicide Act and for measures to enable patients and their representatives to ward off unwanted treatment and vexatious life-support, rather than for an act setting up the paraphernalia of panels considering applications and directing that their decisions be implemented.

It is in consequence no longer so true that "supporters of voluntary euthanasia do not merely want suicide or refusal of treatment or allowing a patient to die. They want the patient dead when he wants to be dead, and they want this accomplished through the physician's agency" (Bandman & Bandman, p. 130). In the great majority of cases, such as those Doris Portwood or Margaret Murray have in mind, the agent would be the patient or, with patients too far gone to act for themselves, the spouse or other close relative or friend. Consider, for example, Lael Wertenbaker's *Death of a Man* (1957) or Derek Humphry's *Jean's Way* (1978). As both would have wished, the prime agent was the spouse: in the former the wife, and in the latter the husband. The only necessary involvement of the medical profession here is to give advice on instruments, maybe to provide the instruments themselves—and not to insist on mounting an all-out campaign to revive the patients.

The desired amendment of the United Kingdom Suicide Act of 1961, an act which already decriminalizes the deed itself, would replace the present general offence of "aiding, abetting, counselling or procuring the suicide of another" by the limited and in fact very rare offense of doing this "with intent to gain or for other selfish or malicious reasons." This amendment would leave the courts to decide, as they so often do elsewhere, when the motives of the assistants were indeed discreditable (Note 7). From a libertarian point of view this suggestion has, unlike any Voluntary Euthanasia Act, the great advantage of specifying not what is legal but what is illegal.

Finally, and with special but not exclusive reference to the other sort of case, in which it is almost bound to be the doctors who would be either killing or letting die, I have a few brief and insufficient words about the absolute sanctity of all (human) life and the idea that killing (people) is always wrong. My suggestion is that, if these so often mentioned principles are to stand any chance of being ultimately acceptable, then both need to be amended in at least two ways.

The first amendment is already accepted almost universally when people think of it. It consists in actually inserting the unstated qualification "innocent." The point is to take account of killing in self-defence and of the execution of those who have committed capital offences. In our terms, people who launch potentially lethal assaults thereby renounce their own claims to the option right to life. Reciprocity is of the essence: just as one person's option right gives rise to the corresponding obligations of all others to respect that right, so violation of the rights of others nullifies the obligations of those others to recognize any corresponding rights vested in the violators (Note 8).

The second amendment consists in adding some indication that what is to be held sacred and inviolate is a person's wish to go on living. This takes account of the enormous, and in almost all contexts crucial, differences between murder and suicide. These are that murderers kill other people, against their will, whereas suicides kill themselves, as they themselves wish. It is perverse and preposterous to characterize suicide, and to condemn it, as self-murder. You might as well denounce intramarital sex as own-spouse adultery.

In the present context the importance of this second amendment is that it attends to those particular human essentials that provide the grounds upon which all claims to universal human rights must be based. It was to these that Blackstone (1825) was referring when, in discussing "the absolute rights of man," he wrote "of man, considered as a free agent, endowed with discernment to know good from evil, and with the power of choosing these measures which appear to him to be most desirable." It was on these same universal features that Thomas Jefferson himself insisted. In Query XIV to the *Notes on the State of Virginia* (1787, 1955), he made various lamentable remarks about blacks, remarks which I shall not repeat, and which would today disqualify him from all elective office. Yet for Jefferson, notwithstanding all these alleged racial deficiencies, blacks (and Indians) certainly do have what it takes to be endowed with the "rights to life, liberty and the pursuit of happiness." Again, it was to these same essential features of people, beings capable of chosing values and objectives for themselves, and of having their own reasons for these choices, that Immanuel Kant (1968) was referring when he laid down that famous but most confused formula: "Act in such a way that you always treat humanity, whether in your own person or in the person of another, never simply as a means, but always at the same time as an end" (p. 94).

It is a temptation to discuss more fully the rationale for the fundamental option rights, and, in particular, to dispose of Kant's own topsy-turvy contention that the respect for persons as self-legislating choosers of their own ends requires that they not choose their own end as an end. I will, instead, conclude by relating that right to die, which I take to be part of the option right to life, to the Hippocratic Oath. This pledge is still often cited as a decisive reason why doctors and other health-care professionals must strive always and by all means to maintain life, irrespective of both the quality of that life and the wishes of its liver. This reason is still frequently flourished, even though nowadays probably only a small minority of doctors outside the ever-expanding socialist bloc do in fact swear that oath. (It is of course outlawed within the socialist bloc precisely because it makes doctors the servants of their patients, rather than of society or the state.)

The relevant sentences of the Hippocratic Oath read: "I will use treatments to help the sick according to my ability and judgment, but never with a view to injury and wrong-doing. I will not give anyone a lethal dose if asked to do so, nor will I suggest such a course (*Hippocrates,* 1959, p. 298). It is obvious that, in the area of today's gerontological concerns, the second and subsidiary undertaking may come into conflict with the primary promise to "use treatments to help the sick according to my ability and judgment."

In such situations it is impossible to keep the oath. Happily, there is no doubt which of the incompatibles should then be preserved. For at the heart of the entire Hippocratic tradition is the ideal of the independent professional, who, always of course within the framework formed by the universal imperatives of moral duty, puts his skills at the service of his patients. So it is quite clear, to me at any rate, that given a more libertarian system of public law, that service must not only exclude forcing unwanted treatment upon those who have asked (either directly or indirectly) to be left alone, but must also include providing instrumental advice on suicide, and maybe the means too, if suicide is the considered wish of their patients.

REFERENCE NOTES

1. Hayek, F. A. *New essays*. London: Routledge and Kegan Paul, 1977, p. 290. Hayek says only that the quote is taken from an old *Encyclopedia of the Social Sciences*. On the substantive issues, see "The Jensen Uproar" in my *Sociology, Equality and Education* (New York: Barnes and Noble, 1976).

2. Bandman, E. L., & Bandman, B. (Eds.). *Bioethics and human rights*. Boston: Little Brown, 1978, Chapter 4.

3. This quote is copied from a report in *The General Practitioner* (London) for 11/26/78. The other comes from the September 1978 issue of that doughtily libertarian magazine *Reason* (Santa Barbara, California).

4. Bandman, E. L., & Bandman, B. (Eds.). *Bioethics and human rights*. Boston: Little Brown, 1978, Chapter 5.

5. See Brownlie, I. (Ed.). *Basic documents of human rights*. Oxford: Clarendon, 1971.

6. My employment of either the single word as an intransitive verb or the affected-sounding gallicism "suicide themselves" is calculated. For the ordinary English expression "commit suicide" is one of those expressions—first noted in Aristotle's *Nicomachean Ethics*, 1107A 8–13—which "already imply badness." Since I do not hold that suicide is always wrong, I deliberately eschew that implication.

7. We owe the precise terms of this suggestion to Tom Parramore, Secretary of our sibling society in Australia.

8. It is here to the point to quote from a now perhaps no longer disfavored sage. A pupil once asked Confucius whether his rule of conduct might not perhaps be epitomized in a single word: "The Master replied, 'Is not "reciprocity" the word?'" See *The Analects*, translated and edited by W. E. Soothill (Taiyuanfu, Shansi: Soothill, 1910), XV §23.

References

Bandman, E. L., Bandman, B. *Bioethics and human rights*. Boston: Little Brown, 1978.

Blackstone, W. *Commentaries on the laws of England*. London: Cadell and Butterworth, 1825.

The Guardian (London). January 20, 1979.

Hippocrates and the fragments of Heracleitus. W. H. S. Jones & E. T. Withington (Ed. & Trans.). Vol. 1. Cambridge, Massachusetts: Harvard University Press, 1959. (The translation quoted is, in fact, my own.)

Humphry, D. *Jean's way*. London: Collins Fontana, 1978.

Jefferson, T. *Notes on the state of Virginia*. W. Peden (Ed.). Chapel Hill: University of North Carolina Press, 1955.

Kant, I. Groundwork of the metaphysic of murals, in H. J. Paton (Trans.), *The moral law*. London: Hutchinson, 1968.

Lincoln, A. *The complete works of Abraham Lincoln* (vol. 1). J. G. Nicolay & J. Hay (Eds.). New York: The Century Company, 1920.

Muir, R., Jr. The opinion of Robert Muir, in the matter of Karen Quinlan: An alleged incompetent. Super A. N. J., Chancery Division, Morris Company, C-201-75, 1975.

Portwood, D. *Common-sense suicide*. New York: Dodd Mead, 1978.

Roe v. Wade. 410 U.S. 113, 93 S. A. 705, 1973.

Wertenbaker, L. *Death of a man*. Boston: Beacon, 1957.

Chapter 8

THE ROLE OF THE FUNERAL DIRECTOR IN CONTEMPORARY SOCIETY

Robert Fulton

In discussing the role of the caretaker of the dead, I think one should first be aware of a certain level of anticipation or even of anxiety that such a discussion generates. I think this is part and parcel of a general tension that is evident when such issues as death and dying are raised. Despite the belief that we have lifted the veil on this taboo topic, there is nevertheless a certain reluctance or uneasiness in addressing it openly.

General avoidance or denial of death, however, is often matched by a strong desire to probe and inquire into all the different aspects of the subject. My mother exemplified this ambivalence toward death as well as anyone. She used to nag my father about preparing his will, for example. On one occasion I overheard her say "Ed, put your paper down; I want to talk about something. We have avoided discussing our deaths long enough. Ed," she said, "whichever one of us dies first, I think I will go live in Florida."

There is a general reluctance to deal with the issues of dying and death, particularly as they relate to the aged. This is surprising when you consider that for the first time in the history of the world the elderly have a virtual monopoly on death: Statistically speaking, it is the elderly who are most likely to die in the United States, and for that matter throughout the industrialized nations of the world. It is critically important that gerontologists in particular recognize this fact and prepare to deal with its implications.

Death, of course, has always been among us, and ultimately all human beings, as well as all living things, die. All life ends in death and all relationships end in separation. Yet we resist these ideas today, just as the Neanderthals did 60,000 years ago. Even those primitive people ceremoniously laid out and buried their dead with symbols and artifacts suggesting a belief in an afterlife. Since the time those graves were dug at Shanidar, Iraq, humankind has had ambivalent feelings about death, and about the human corpse. This is evident in the fact that we show great respect for the dead human body even as we try to avoid it.

On the one hand we believe death is purposeful—the will of God. On the other hand it is viewed as integral to our biological existence, and natural. From one perspective, death is only one experience in a series of experiences we can expect as humans, while from another perspective, there is only one life—and one death—and of the rest we know nothing. So from the time of Shanidar to the present one can observe a mixture of responses to the significance of death. And, as I have observed, associated with these ideas and reactions is an ambivalence toward the dead human body.

A cross-cultural view of the world will show, for instance, that while some societies abandon the body at the time of death as well as the place of death itself, other societies literally ingest the corpse. So from abandoning the body to eating it, we are made aware of the remarkable array of human responses to death.

The Egyptians embraced the idea of reincarnation by elaborately preparing the body in expectation of the soul's long journey and ultimate return. The Cairo Museum displays an embalming board that is over 46 centuries old. What that tells us, if nothing else, is that the idea of immortality, of humankind's belief in the persistence of existence, is historic.

To understand the role of the contemporary funeral director it has to be placed in such an historical and meaningful setting. Over the centuries, of course, the role of layer-out-of-the-dead or handler-of-the-dead has been assumed by different persons whose status has varied greatly—not only throughout Western European society but in other cultures also.

Historically, and indeed up until the present day, Judaism has seen in the Hevra Kaddisha's, voluntary laying out of the dead, the most honorific gesture that one person can make toward another. It was, and is, considered the greatest of gifts—the greatest mitzvah—to lay out the dead. Again, the root of this attitude can be found in the belief that there is a spiritual risk in approaching or touching the dead human body. So again we observe an approach-avoidance relationship with the human corpse that is almost schizophrenic. We view it as something to be respected or revered at the same time that we attempt to avoid it or put it away.

In many religious communities throughout the world, mutilation of the corpse for the purpose of an autopsy is not tolerated. This attitude toward the sanctity of the dead human body is evidenced over thousands of years, from the time when the Egyptian priest-surgeon responsible for embalming the pharaohs risked physical harm as a result of what was considered a necessary but nevertheless sacrilegious act.

Among the Thlinget, a west coast Canadian tribe, the body is avoided so assiduously that its care is given over to another group entirely. The Thlinget, in turn, reciprocate when necessary.

In France, since the medieval period, the few embalmers have all been physicians, whereas in America the role of embalmer appeared at the time of the Civil War with little or no academic or professional tradition behind him. Consequently, the status of the embalmer or layer-out-of-the-dead in America has been at best ambiguous, while at worst is has approximated the status of a public executioner.

The emergence of the contemporary American embalmer, mortician, or, more recently, funeral director, is a consequence of many different forces. But it can primarily be attributed to the burgeoning of our industrial, technological society since World War I, with its emphasis on the division of labor, specialization, and efficiency. Urbanization, secularization, social mobility and family nucleation have also played their part in seeing that the care of the dying as well as the dead in America became the responsibility of someone outside the family circle.

A survey I conducted some years ago found that while some funeral homes on the east coast have been in continuous operation for over 200 years, the average funeral home in the United States had been in existence about 55 years. Over this relatively short time the questions: who die, where do they die, and from what, have changed dramatically. Most deaths today are among the elderly rather than the young; they die in the hospital rather than at home; and they die from chronic and degenerative illnesses like heart disease and cancer rather than from infectious and contagious diseases. These demographic changes, among others, are integral to a discussion of the appropriate role of the contemporary American funeral director.

The different studies that I have conducted about death, funerals, and funeral directors have shown that in the last few decades, and particularly since World War II, criticism of funeral practices in the United States has been loud, persistent, and ubiquitous. At this very moment, the Federal Trade Commission is preparing a series of recommendations based on their investigations and hearings that will attempt to define not only the procedures to be followed by funeral directors, but also the parameters of his services.

Without going into the specific issues at this time, I would like to spell out the social and attitudinal environment in which funerals are conducted today and in which funeral directors play their part, so that we might have a better sense of what they, as well as we, are about in the latter half of the twentieth century.

Generally speaking, in the eyes of many people the funeral director's role is in conflict with some of our religious values. To many, the emphasis he places on the body appears to take priority over the spirit. The funeral director, moreover, is charged with usurping the function of the clergy and presuming upon the role of the family, while the funeral itself is said to be held for its own sake with little regard to the needs or wishes of the bereaved. There is also great concern over the funeral director's alleged efforts to promote expensive and elaborate funerals while urging viewing and embalming upon grieving families. All of this seen as contrary to our traditional beliefs and practices.

And yet, for good or ill, the services provided by funeral directors reflect the manner and direction in which American society has moved in most other public services as well. We have turned to the modern funeral home and the contemporary funeral director for services that once were the responsibility and right of the family. But this is true, as we know, of many other features of American life as well.

Any analysis of funeral practices, however, must begin with the recognition of the regional, ethic, and religious variability found in America. Although there are now 22,000 funeral homes in the United States—an overabundance according to some—it must be recognized that like the small town with its different churches, American funeral homes serve different religious, cultural, and ethnic groups, as well as different social classes across many different regions of the United States. This not only makes for an apparent redundancy of facilities and services, it also makes it difficult to speak accurately about an average American funeral. In one community, moreover, there may be found a funeral home that has been in existence for three or four generations under the same family management, while in another community there may be a branch of a large conglomerate or funeral chain. These and other conditions affect the general situation and compel us to recognize the factors of variability and change that bear on this social phenomenon.

For instance, as I have mentioned, elderly persons now have the greatest probability of dying in the United States. Last year 70% of the persons who died were over 65. Less than 6% of the persons who died were under 15. By contrast, at the turn of the century children made up over half of all deaths, yet represented only one-third of the population. The elderly, on the other hand, made up 4% of the population and accounted for 17% of the deaths. Today, however, the elderly represent 11% of the population and account for more than two-thirds of all deaths.

The elderly, as we know, more often than not die away from home, away from their families, often isolated and alone. Most gerontologists are aware, as well as concerned, about the changing sets of relationships implicit in these developments as they affect family contacts, family commitments, and family continuity. It means, fundamentally, if the recent study we conducted at the University of Minnesota is at all an indicator, that attitudes toward the dying as well as the dead are changing in America—and changing significantly.

Our study, for instance, suggests that responses and reactions to death are now both variable and in flux, and that these changes are a function of changes in religious beliefs, social class and mobility, and family relationships. We found that while there are many basic similarities between the responses of survivors toward the death of a family member, the degree and nature of the relationships can be crucial to the specific reaction reported. That is, the response of a parent to the death of a son or daughter, or of a wife to the death of a husband, can be radically different from the response of an adult son or daughter to the death of an elderly parent.

But as we have observed, not only are most people who die elderly, but they are a burgeoning age group in our society. Today over 23 million persons are over 65. Of this group 7 million are over 75, and persons over 100 number now in the thousands. We also realize that America is a highly urbanized, mobile, and secular society, and that our families are increasingly nuclear in form and function. The death of an elderly person in a hospital or nursing home after a long illness is quite different from the sudden, unexpected death of a child by accident in his own home. How one responds, how one acts, or what is to be done with the body take on a different significance in these different contexts.

In San Diego in 1978, one sixth of all deaths was handled in the following manner: After the death, an organization called the Telephase Society was notified and arrangements were made to deliver the body from the place of death to a crematorium in an unmarked van. Encased in a rubberized bag, the body was then cremated, and the ashes were scattered or placed in a cardboard container for later disposition. A bill for this service was subsequently mailed to the surviving spouse or other responsible party.

Practically nothing is known of the survivors' emotional reactions to these deaths, or what arrangements, if any, were made to memorialize the dead. Nor do we know anything of the survivor's manner of grief.

We do know, however, from our research at the University of Minnesota, that the 40- to 60-year-old children of elderly persons who died reported muted or limited feelings of grief at the time of the death. In fact, a few men in the study reported that upon the deaths of their fathers they felt in no way bereaved. Nor did they commemorate their deaths in any way. For some of the respondents, their attitude was that their fathers had lived out their lives and now they were over. Any service or response other than the immediate disposition of the body was viewed as unnecessary or inappropriate. One respondent even wrote that, as far as he was concerned, his dead father's body was "just a hunk of meat." In our sample persons such as this responded to their loss in as minimal a way as possible. While responses like these were in a distinct minority, nevertheless they augur an increase of such sentiments and remind us again of the varied and problematical responses to death.

In the face of these and other developments still emergent in the United States, the question of the role of the contemporary funeral director is increasingly relevant to us all and particularly to gerontologists. The answer or answers to that question, however, are both difficult and contingent.

There is tremendous variability in the response to loss by death. Death doesn't mean the same thing to all people. How one reacts to the death of another depends upon many different personal and social factors. What is the appropriate disposition of a dead human body? What should we expect of a funeral director or of a funeral? As I mentioned, in the San Diego area one of six bodies is being handled in a most direct and unceremonious manner. But the general practice across the country reflects degrees of relationship and levels of feeling and expectations different from what is occurring in this particular section of the country.

What is the role of the funeral director under these circumstances, given that we are a highly secularized society and generally shielded from the more unpleasant conditions and experiences of life? Moreover, we run away from death as well as the place of death. Citizens in our society, as in many other societies, characteristically display an impulse to leave the place of death, to move and withdraw from friends and relatives. What is the role of the funeral director when we also consider, that in addition to such specific behavior, that one of every five families moves every year? What is the role of the funeral director when our survey of almost 600 survivors showed that less than 15% reported being contacted by a clergyman or other professional person following the death of a family member? What is the role of the funeral director in a highly urbanized community when great numbers of people live in isolated or nucleated states of existence?

What is the role of a funeral director when the general population is increasingly educated to live in our highly techno-logical society, while the funeral director's education consists generally of a high school education plus two years of practical training? Although it is improving, the training the funeral direc-tor receives is probably not in keeping with the training of most of the younger members of the community, who sooner or later will seek out his services.

What is the role of the funeral director in a society in which the clergy views him as offending many of their cherished beliefs and traditions? To associate the contemporary funeral with his-toric Egyptian funeral customs, as some funeral directors do, does violence to traditional Christian theology. For a funeral director to participate in a Catholic service in the morning and a Protestant service in the afternoon is acceptable and desirable from an ecumenical point of view; nevertheless, for many clergy-men the funeral director's acceptance of all faiths as spiritually equal by implication casts doubt on the presumed spiritual effica-cy of their rites and rituals, as well as on the presumed primacy of sanctity of their respective faiths. For these and other reasons, the two functionaries most significantly associated with the disposi-tion of the dead in American society are at odds with one another by the very nature of their commitments and obligations.

But at the same time the funeral director is not wholly a businessman—a salesman. We must remember that at the same time we cast him into a macabre role or make him the object of droll humor, he also performs a mitzvah—albeit for a fee, like the doctor and the lawyer. His function parallels the traditional ser-vice of the Hevra Kaddisha—of laying out the community's dead. He is performing a task that we ourselves choose not to do, and he does so in a manner that conveys the respect we reserve for the dead. As a consequence he takes on a sacerdotal function, a priestly role, while at the same time he is a merchandizer of coffins and other accoutrements of the grave.

His role, therefore, is by its very nature contradictory. This contradiction becomes most clear when we realize that funeral directors are the only "businessmen," or persons without professional degrees, who are permitted to attend to a naked human body. There are exceptions of course—the artist is one—but for all intents and purposes the funeral director shares a sacerdotal function with the priest and physician, and to the extent that he does, his role is unique to American occupations and professions. Therein lies much of the confusion and conflict associated with our assessment of him as a functionary of the dead.

What role, then, can we assign to him when we question his motives and are confused about his rightful tasks? How difficult it is to attribute to him good intentions when at the same time we are ever fearful that he will exploit his client's grief for his own gain, particularly since we believe that one of the greatest things that you can do for a fellow human being is to offer help—without expecting compensation—when he or she has suffered the loss of a loved one.

These reasons, historically contradictory reasons, evoke so much emotion that we find the role of the American funeral director one of conflict. Yet we must ask ourselves, who is going to help at the time of death? Our surveys show that there are very few professional persons who now help the bereaved. Who is going to be at the home of the bereaved first? Who is going to advise the grief-stricken? Who is going to inform the widow of her rights? There are very few sociologists or psychologists available. When a person dies in the hospital, the doctor views his job as over; so does the nurse. Only now with the rise of the hospice movement do we see a preliminary and tentative attempt to respond to a few of the issues implicit in my questions.

What we must come to recognize is that the funeral director has been, and is, an important caregiver in the American community. We must come to appreciate that inherent in his role and intrinsic to his skills and experience, are social opportunities and individual talents that must be channeled and employed even more. They must be galvanized and harnessed by the community so that the services he provides and the skills he possesses can be utilized to their fullest.

What are the skills and services that the funeral director possesses and that the health care field must look at and reassess?

First, of all the different persons in the community to whom one can turn at the time of death, the funeral director is not only the most visible, but more often than not the most available. Simply, it is his business. That is what he is paid to do, and the fact that members of his family may have been serving the same community for two or three generations provides a basis of trust and security that is not readily appreciated or available among other members of a community's health care network. The studies of Charles Binger at the Langely Porter Institute and Colin Parkes at Harvard have shown that following a death the person who was designated as being helpful or an important social resource to the bereaved was the family funeral director.

There are many reasons for these findings. Experience, for one thing: The funeral director was frequently the only knowledgeable person who would speak about the dead person or who was relatively comfortable discussing the death with the bereaved. By way of contrast, it is reported that some nursing homes whisk dying patients out of the home to avoid the taint and stigma of a death. In Minneapolis, for example, one particular nursing home has advertised that the reason there was always a room available for occupancy was that residents got well and went home. In short, when we look clinically and less critically at funerals and funeral directors, we recognize that the person who is often identified as most knowledgeable about the problems associated with a death, who knows what to do and is helpful and supportive to the bereaved, is the funeral director.

Let us consider for a moment the attitudes toward death and dying of gerontologists, academicians, doctors, nurses, and other concerned members of the network of health care in the community. On the one hand, they are profoundly committed to the idea of education and training, and all of the other things basic to good council and advice. On the other hand, they recognize that when someone dies their own avoidance of death, their shyness or anxiety about it, do not allow them as professional persons to intervene and support survivors any more than the neighbor or friend across the street. This observation and the recurring question—what to do about death?—brings me back again to the important role the American funeral director plays in our lives.

I would argue, moreover, that if we would begin to see him as a member of the community mental health team, we would recognize that he is virtually an untapped resource. And that if we begin to open up lines of communication with him in our capacity as health care practitioners, as members of the clergy, and as community social workers, we will discover that there is much to be gained and little to be lost in the face of the great challenge that death presents to us all.

REFERENCES

Binger, C. M., et al. Childhood leukemia: Emotional impact on patient and family. *The New England Journal of Medicine* 1969, p. 417.

Owen, G., et al. Death at a Distance: A Study of Survivors, (Minneapolis: Center for Death Education and Research, 1948) 50 pgs., unpublished.

Parkes, C. M., Glick, I. O., and Weiss, R. S. *The first year of bereavement.* New York: John Wiley and Sons, 1974, pp. 97–117.

Chapter 9

THE EXPERIENCE OF DYING

Daniel G. O'Hare

It is not abstract theory that concerns me, but rather the critical need for an entire educative process designed to confront the issue of death and the understanding of it. There is a lamentable absence of adequate preparation for death in contemporary society, especially before the emotionally charged, physically impairing, and psychologically draining period immediately preceding death, especially a death that follows a long and painful illness. People must learn to anticipate and, moreover, to appreciate the certainty of death as a precondition to dealing with it.

Simultaneously, even while involved in a theoretical reflection on death, it is possible for each of us to become aware of the more immediate and pressing needs of the terminally ill, those who are dying now, and particularly those for whom the remote preparation was inadequate, but for whom the reality is now present. The situation of the terminally ill will not only permit us an opportunity to develop a facility for caring for those who are dying, but can encourage us to raise our own questions about our own death.

It is the disposition of our approach, however, that is of critical importance. How *do* we initiate an understanding of the experience of dying? How *can* we begin to appreciate what factors operate in, what pressures can be brought to bear on, and what misconceptions can cloud the process of dying? Borrowing from my own philosophical background and adopting an Aristotelian precedent, I suggest that in the absence of personal experience, we discover what it is to die by observing the person who is dying. But a serious caution must be introduced at this point. There is the danger of self-exception, of lifting oneself out of the situation in question. It is a psychological maneuver of which we are all capable, and unfortunately with regard to death, one repeatedly engaged in even by those who are directly involved in the care of the dying.

Just who, then, is the person who is dying? Is it the person admitted last week, the person who is being diagnosed this week, or the person who will die next week? Is it always just some other person? Will it always be just some other person? Or is it also you and I? Are not we too the ones who are dying? To delve more deeply into the experience of dying through participation in the death of someone else, we need to enter that situation not only as caretakers, but more fundamentally as the unique individuals we are, individuals concerned about death in our own lives. We come asking not merely academic questions about death in general, but existential and personal questions about our own death in particular.

As we examine some of the factors, some of the pressures, and some of those misconceptions that surround the experience of dying, we must reflect on the individual who is facing death, not only as the other but also as our own self, for we too are the ones who are dying. It would be relatively easy to utilize the following as a catalog of the stages and traumas that nameless and faceless dying people undergo. It would not be difficult to extract from what will follow a compact set of guidelines or a set of instructions for a task we have to perform for someone else. It is possible that in raising the question of our own dying, we will be more acutely sensitive to the needs of those around us who are dying, and I believe that in avoiding our own death, we will find it increasingly difficult to deal with the deaths of others. Thus in a calm and reflective manner, rather than in an emotionally charged state, we can begin to consider the experience of dying.

In the phenomenological investigation of death, it is essential that we pay attention to the personal and societal backgrounds that affect, manipulate, and to some extent control our response to the prospect of dying. The following is an attempt to illuminate the environment in which we dare to raise our question about death, for it is in this environment that we encounter our first difficulties.

First, as individuals we do not know much about death, and we do not have—or, perhaps more correctly, do not use—opportunities to expand that knowledge. Yet there is death in all our lives: We have all undergone permanent transitions, have been faced with final separations, and have come to irreversible terminations. Rarely, however, do we recognize the dying in all those experiences: the finality, the fear and misgivings, and the letting go. We hesitate facing the passage that has occurred, fail to integrate the experience, leap to another preoccupation, and leave the situation without expanding our understanding. We rob ourselves of a fundamental human experience and move through life unable to cope with the rhythm of joining and separating which characterizes living and which forecasts the ultimate separation in dying. The manner with which we contend with these experiences throughout life is a fairly accurate indicator of the manner in which we will face death.

Given the opportunity, we frequently do not want to talk about death; at times, we would rather not even hear about it. Couched in the self-exception mentioned previously, we presume that "it" will always happen to someone else, or, if indeed it will happen to me, it will only be in the vague and distant future. We are much too busy now, much too involved, much too needed, and much too responsible to and for others to consider dying! Particularly with the decrease in infant mortality, extension of life expectancy, greater control over formerly catastrophic illnesses, and—quite significantly—the institutionalizing of dying, we have less and less firsthand experience with death. This distancing not only robs us of an intimacy with that fundamental human experience but, even subconsciously, enables repression and denial of its reality to continue and to be reinforced.

It should also be obvious that searching for scientific or legal definitions, the biological data of death, is somewhat misguided, if not evasive, as an attempt to explain and understand the experience. For only a moment's consideration of the death of someone with whom we are in one way or another involved, of someone we love, or of our own death, points to the fact that we are not talking about a purely biological or merely physiological phenomenon. The gradual ebbing of life in someone else, someone we love, is not just a biological process anymore than my own death, and all it entails, can be described in legal terms. There is another dimension containing all the factors of our unique personhood: the social, the emotional, and the spiritual. These are important considerations for each of us, but considerations that are not addressed in legal or scientific terms.

For all the less than pleasant aspects which frequently are connected with it, for all the frustration and disappointment which creeps in occasionally, my life is still precious to me. Of course, I could wish to be elsewhere, with other people, doing other things, but even that points to how much I want to hold onto my life, improve it, and cherish it.

The tragedy is that there is a holding onto life that is actually a holding *back* from life, a fear of dying that has resulted in a fear of living. Regardless of our personal estimation of death or our beliefs concerning what it forecasts, to live life more fully we need to face the fear, deal with the frustration, contend with the guilt, and acknowledge the element of incompleteness that death introduces into our lives. For it is only in this way, as relatively free of communication-hampering pain and illness as possible, that we can begin to calm our fear, quell our frustration, not be consumed with guilt, and set about the task of completing our unfinished business so that life might go on. Such a life is appreciated more fully and lived more deeply.

If it is true that understanding any aspect of life enriches our understanding of its possibilities, then an increased understanding of death can enhance life's creative possibilities and establish priorities. Facing death, few questions are as important—or as liberating—as "What is important now?" While I am certainly willing to admit the ultimate ineffability of death, I am also convinced that the one response to death most doomed to failure is the attempt to ignore it. No advance whatsoever will be made in either confronting or contending with death as long as it is seen only as something completely unnatural, totally abrupt, and surprisingly ending my life.

Regrettably, however, this view of death is characteristic of modern mankind; and the more that one is unwilling to face one's death, the more one is unable to face one's life. In running from death, do we also run from life? Even the most contemporary theater, literature, and other forms of human expression constantly echo the theme that we live our lives without reflecting upon their quality and purpose. When that life draws to a close, we view it as vacuous and devoid of meaning, which in turn renders death more absurd and horrifying. We race through life and forget how to live. For many of us, long before dying is a problem, living is a problem. Thus we need to contend with death, and we need to contend with it now. In the final analysis, the fear of immobilization and the threat of annihilation are only increased as a result of evasive techniques.

It is tragically ironic that the sole event that we can anticipate with certitude is also the one we find ourselves least prepared for and, consequently, most often incapacitated by. We can atttempt to ignore it, we can drown ourselves in self-pity, and we can smoulder in anger, but, ironically, those responses only destroy the quality of life we are presumably anxious to preserve. To choose life and live it most fully involves facing death. Unless we face death in a way that will at least give us an opportunity to come to terms with it, the fear and anxiety that eventually overtake us can be both demoralizing and debilitating. Of particular importance is the need to separate the fears of the process of dying from the question of death itself, lest these become unnecessarily confused or clouded. While certainly related, they are not the same issue.

A second problem in facing death is that even the individual who might be so inclined, the individual who is seeking to understand the meaning of the experience of death in his or her life, finds himself or herself in a culture that does not support or encourage that effort, but rather imposes taboos, subtly or otherwise. In what is now a nearly perfect caricature of denial, it has been noted that it is peculiarly un-American to die! Bizarre as that sounds, in a society that places so much value on constant vitality and such a premium on perpetual youthfulness, death simply has no place.

My experience in both a leper colony in India and a hospice in England has led me to believe that each of those cultures was more exposed to, and more comfortable with, the natural pattern of the life cycle. Birth and death were more apparent in each, and the passage of life was more pronounced since there were fewer mechanisms employed to obliterate it. Most assuredly, people died in each of those cultures, but that experience was not set apart, not removed, from the context of life in general. It is questionable progress, in my opinion, if a society is geared to conditioning its members to avoid whatever is not concertedly youthful or aggressively vital. It produces an atmosphere fabricated on denial.

Reflect for a moment on what we do with the old or the sick in our society. Where do we put them? Why? Just for them and for their care? I wonder. Sequestering the aged and the sick not only places such individuals in a state of loneliness, stripping them of their self-worth, contributing to their fears of becoming useless and burdensome, and forcing them to face death feeling unsupported, if not unloved. But in removing the reminders of our own contingency, it also allows us to pursue the myth of our deathlessness. The lamentable result of this evasive technique is that both the young and the old, the well and the unwell, the living and the dying, are radically incomplete in their experience and sharing of life.

There are additional societal complications that render the experience of death increasingly difficult both for those who are dying and those who suffer with or care for them. A particularly oppressive factor in the deaths of those whose illnesses have been long and painful is that as a culture we have been seduced by the appeal of the instant and automatic. Not only do we know that it is possible to travel at supersonic speeds, to view events as they happen in other parts of the world, and to prepare entire meals in a matter of minutes in a microwave oven, but we have been led to believe that anything that can be done, can and should be done quickly. Speed and efficiency are singularly important values. This is a problem particularly indigenous to American society.

And even for those of us who claim to prefer a more leisurely pace, the societal impact is there. We grow easily impatient and ultimately frustrated with what cannot be so quickly and easily accomplished.

The prospect of a long illness, terminating in death, is not quickly or easily accommodated. It is not uncommon, therefore, that the adjustment to death, the acknowledgment of what has occurred, and the necessity of facing the pain involved are often repressed. If we can't do it quickly, we won't do it.

I have grown suspicious of apparently rapid and total adjustments to death. Mourning is therapeutic, and grief is not the trauma, but the healing process following death. Grief must be public to be shared and shared to be diminished. When such manifestations of grief are absent, I am left wondering if an individual has in fact adjusted to the separation and loss or repressed dealing with it. In the face of our subtle coercion to accomplish things quickly and our not so subtle pressure to be "with it" and not appear extraordinary, we may have attempted to adjust so quickly or completely that the result was a repression rather than a confronting of the loss involved.

In a manner similar to our seduction by the appeal of the automatic, we have also become convinced of the myth of the totally resolvable. We imagine that, either as individuals or in concert with others, we can solve everything. We have made and continue to make incredible advances to sustain and improve the quality of life. Our faith in the possibilities of scientific and technological progress is boundless. Is death just one more malady to be conquered?

The irony is that we are introduced to this myth very early in life, and we are introduced to it through television. Whole generations have grown up witnessing endless scenarios of the most complex and tragic human situations portrayed on the television screen, and, what is more important, they have also seen all those problems neatly and completely solved in 60 minutes or less. That has an impact on our ability to sustain the incomplete or the unresolved, a subtle influence on our ability to endure, for ourselves or for others, the lengthy, painful process that often precedes death.

Geared to completing things quickly and controlling them

maximally, we are disconcerted by whatever cannot be done immediately, whatever will not be controlled completely, or whatever simply will not eventually go away, and death is the paradigm for all that. While we are given to finding solutions that are neat and discrete, death raises the element of the mysterious, the protracted, and the enduring in life. If unable to cope with that, we turn to denial; and when confronted with death, we have tried to make it unreal.

As I mentioned previously, in any society that increasingly views the handling of even nonviolent and nonabrupt death as the responsibility of institutions, widespread inexperience has contributed to the phenomena of hesitation and denial. Even much of the contemporary interest in death and dying— although certainly beneficial primarily in raising the issues—has tended to over-popularization and over-dramatization at the cost of a somewhat superficial treatment of the question of death. We can still talk about it without letting it touch our lives. For some it is even possible to deal with death without letting it touch their lives.

Despite our own lack of understanding as individuals (my first point), and the apparent inability of society to provide acknowledgment and supportive assistance (my second point), death eventually looms on the no longer distant horizon for everyone. As I used to remark in England, with all due respect to the monarchy, death remains the most democratic experience of mankind. While that is perfectly obvious, perfectly natural, and therefore perfectly necessary in life, it is not something that is met with great resoluteness.

My third contention is that even those who face death as the result of a long and painful illness are not assured of discovering proper care and support, even from those who manifestly engage in such care. Dying persons are often unable to contend resolutely with their own questions if unassisted, and coming from a society that has forced internalization of those questions and repression of their attendant fears, the terminally ill face a desperately lonely and difficult prospect. It is unfortunate, but nonetheless true, that the impact of societal taboos can reach the medical realm also. Medical personnel are still products of their own culture, and those closest to the terminally ill are not always those most able, or even most willing, to offer support.

Consider the following incident: A few years ago I had the privilege of touring a major cancer research institute, and had the opportunity to meet informally with doctors, nurses, social workers, and other medical personnel who function as a team in patient care. In the course of the conversation I asked about the specifics of their team approach to the care of the terminal patient. I was abruptly advised that "terminal" was not used to describe any patient in that institution. Rather, the doctor said, they were "advanced" or perhaps "chronically" ill. I yielded to the correction, but the essence of my question did remain, and I pursued it. In the ensuing description of various "operative procedures," bloodless language in itself, a physician remarked that he considered death to be the ultimate insult to his expertise. My efforts to discern the nature of that insult failed, and I received no response to my question whether he viewed all healing as physical. I was concerned to know if the completion of physical treatment would necessitate the withdrawal of nonphysical supportive attention.

There are obviously physicians whose sensitivity is not only a source of comfort and assurance to their patients, but a deeper testimony to their own humanity. I am certain, however, that the attitude expressed by that gentleman was not unlike that of many other people and, interestingly enough, of some people who are dealing directly with those who are dying. It is an attitude that forecasts no decrease in anxiety for those who are approaching death. In administering *care, caring* is also necessary, a caring that penetrates beneath the level of what we can do to the level of who we are. Throughout the mechanics of care, there should be a consistency of caring, and, indeed, the gradual cessation of care as treatment should not signal the breakdown of caring as a human response.

Given the personal and cultural background that I have outlined, it should be obvious that the terminally ill person finds himself or herself in a situation, a whole process, for which there has been little or no preparation. The approach of death is an overwhelming experience for most people. Neither their personal nor societal background has permitted or encouraged, or even seen a value in remote and objective preparation for death. But now, despite the lack of understanding, the lack of preparation, and the lack of support in achieving either, the possibility of death has become an imminent probability. Now the question is focused into the experience. It is not unusual for a wide range of feelings and emotions to flood to the surface of one's consciousness: shock, fear, anger, resentment, sorrow, and a host of others depending on the individual's circumstances. Added to this can be the horror and isolation forced on the dying person by his or her feelings of rejection by and estrangement from others, whether or not these feelings are grounded in reality. These are not the only reactions possible, but obviously the more difficult to deal with and those that create a greater challenge for people engaged in caring. If such feelings are frequently in evidence in the experience of dying, learning to deal with them is potentially advantageous both to those who are dying and to those who assist that process.

My own experience with the dying is that throughout the process they wish to be viewed, considered, and treated as a *person*, as the *unique person* each of us is. I suspect that my feelings about my own death will be the same. The stigma that surrounds the prospect of death, however, often makes this desire very difficult to achieve. The pattern of life can be completely altered; even family and close friends can withdraw, and the individual can be viewed as an occupied bed, a case, a statistic. When most in need of support and concern, the deep human intimacy that characterizes our most significant relationships, the dying person can be made to feel his or her difference most sharply, most painfully. "I still want to be treated as a normal person," is a direct and haunting quote from a young woman whom I visited near her death. In various ways I have heard her concern voiced by others: Don't leave me; don't ignore me; don't be afraid to be around me just because I am dying!

The focus has to be on the person as person. This is especially important for medical personnel. A delicate balance must be struck between performing necessary functions for a *patient* and caring for a *person*. Would you want, or permit, the care and treatments you order; would you like to receive the bedbath you give; would the food you serve satisfy your own hunger; and would the level of conversation you engage in sustain you through long, lonely hours in a hospital bed? Would you want your bed surrounded by impersonal but efficient or passive observers, or by active and interested participants in your life? That attempted focusing on the person as person is the only assurance that dignity will be either achieved or maintained. More than the performing of necessary functions, the preservation of dignity demands becoming a "presence," a warm, caring human presence, in the life of the person who is dying. In the absence of that attempt, individual dignity and respect can quickly vanish. Even minimal dignity is difficult to maintain in an institutional setting where you are stripped, tagged, probed, and told to urinate on demand.

An effort should be made to minimize those things that tend to separate us from those who are dying. Such factors include the physical environment, as well as our psychological or emotional disposition. Our powerlessness or lack of control in any situation, intensified for those who are dying, is only multiplied in an environment in which we feel estranged and unfamiliar. Unfortunately, we have come to view the most natural setting for care and nurturing, the home, as an unnatural setting for sickness and death.

In the final analysis there are situations in life that are beyond our control, but that does not mean that we cannot address them, that does not mean that we cannot work through them, particularly with the support of those we love. People need to talk, people want to talk, and that means that someone else has to be willing to listen. Although I believe that we have to respect the pace of the individual, which means that we cannot force someone to talk about dying, the reverse is also true: We should not prohibit someone from talking. It is grossly unfair and insulting to deny any individual the opportunity to talk out his or her hopes and fears. In my own work I have found that, difficult as it might be to initiate such a conversation with a dying individual, the resultant experience is one of great liberation. Now the problem is out in the open; now we can begin to deal with it. Particularly in those situations where such conversations never took place, I have consistently noticed a guilt manifested by those who survive.

Although it is certainly an unfortunate extreme never to discuss death with the dying, it may also be another unbearable extreme to discuss it too soon or too openly. Death admits of no more clarity than life, and it is often difficult to discuss situations in life. If a risk needs to be taken, however, I would risk in favor of initiating such a conversation, encouraging those who are dying that there are people who are willing both to talk and to listen. We need to allow rage, our own and others, to surface. If we can become instantly irritated when we are caught by a red light, miss our bus or train to work, see another car pull into the parking space we just spotted, and at all the ultimately insignificant daily crises, then we should certainly be permitted, if not encouraged, to vent our strongest feelings about death. In surfacing those feelings, we can begin to deal with them. What price silence? Grief, guilt, frustration, and the concern over unfinished business can all be addressed. While these feelings cannot be completely obliterated, dealing with them can permit us to deal with others, clearing the path for deeper communication. Being truly present to the person facing death can only come about in an atmosphere of trust, in which the need for privacy is clearly respected, and when there is a willingness to accomplish what I refer to as "getting inside the boundaries" of the dying.

Trust is an important element, a precious commodity for someone who is anxious to share his or her deepest hopes and fears about dying, and it cannot be toyed with. It is difficult to achieve, easy to lose, and even more difficult to regain. Trust is built on honesty and humility. People who are threatened need to be able to trust someone. Lack of honesty results in lack of trust, and communication breaks down. In my own relative lack of medical knowledge, I have found myself frequently at an advantage with a dying person when I have admitted my ignorance. I have found that it is possible to encourage a person or win his or her confidence by an admission of ignorance and a subsequent willingness to find answers. In such a climate, the dying person genuinely feels that there is "someone on my side."

In dealing with the dying, particularly in the institutional setting, I have learned to be sensitive to the need for privacy. It is a privacy not to be confused with modesty. It is, rather, another plea to concentrate on the person amidst all the trappings of institutionalization. The patient needs to know that what he or she says and feels is both respected and protected.

Most of us want to look well, to feel and act healthy, and we are most pleased when those with whom we deal are also looking, acting, and feeling well. The awesome truth is that the terminally ill person cannot always do all of these things. Eventually he or she will be able to manage none of them. It is precisely then that a continued respect for and interest in the individual must be demonstrated. Such a concentration on the person cuts through all the accumulated paraphernalia of treatment. It is the privacy of devoting time exclusively to the individual on the other side of all that paraphernalia. It demands that those caring do not do so in an expeditious manner, and it also means that in the intimacy of a relationship with a dying person, disproportionate concern about showing emotion should be avoided. Can you afford to behave as though totally indifferent? Can you be totally un-affected by the impending death of someone with whom you have a relationship? Will your inability to enter deeply into such a relationship be the result of your anxiety over demonstrating emotion? What strenuous restraints will that place on the indi-viduals who are dying? Can we ask them not to display emotion?

Few of us have had the experience of entertaining our friends in a bedroom while surrounded by other beds filled with every manner of very ill people attached to intravenous tubes, monitoring facilities, drainage bags, and oxygen machines. It is, at best, a situation that appears designed to inhibit deep interper-sonal relating. When the dying person cannot move out from behind those barriers to communicate, it is necessary that some-one be willing to move in, to address the person behind all that machinery.

Finally, trust and sensitivity for privacy can be brought to fruition through what I have defined as "getting within the boundaries" of the person who is dying.

Based on my experience in the leper colony, where enforced isolation and lack of human support were the rule, I reflected on the terminally ill person, the person behind bedrails. I pondered the "Do not disturb" signs, restricted visiting hours, frequently with restricted visitors, and I realized that terminally ill persons are the twentieth century's Western lepers. We build a wall around them and stand safely outside it.

To the chagrin of endless nurses, I begin visits with people who are dying by lowering the bedrails and sitting on their beds. It is a small sign, but it says I am willing to get into that lonely little world. Touching says I am not afraid of you; your death won't contaminate me. Talking may wear the very tired individual, but it produces a welcome sleep brought on from satisfied exhaustion rather than narcotics. Is all that draining? Most definitely. Is it difficult? Most assuredly. It is all a hedge against the alternative— dying alone and afraid.

In some, although certainly not all cases, I have found that there has been a real conversion, a movement toward acceptance, and a letting go. It is a humbling experience to witness an individual bringing closure to his or her life with dignity and peace. But I have witnessed that only where there was an atmosphere in which talking and listening, trusting and respecting, and caring were possible.

As individuals and as a society, we need death education. We need to ask our questions and deal with our feelings now in a supportive context of love and concern, all of which means that we must decide to face death before it faces us.

Chapter 10

SPIRITUAL WELL-BEING OF THE DYING

David O. Moberg

Sociologists of religion are typically more inclined to comment on
the data that illustrate the secularization of society than to recognize the significance of major strands of sacralization in modern,,
industrialized, enlightened Western civilization. That death has
been secularized can hardly be denied. Historical changes reflect
the process. As Schneidman (1977) has indicated,

> . . . over the past generation or two there has been a
> tremendous secularization of death. Nowadays people die
> ascetically in antiseptic hospitals rather than aesthetically in
> their homes. The physician has replaced the priest; the
> doctor is today's magician who has the power to extend life,
> our new escort from this vale of tears. The funeral industry
> directs the forms of mourning, ushering us from burial to
> bereavement (p. 72).

Survey data also support the conclusion that religious beliefs
associated with death become more secular and "scientized" with
the maturing of young adults. Children's conceptions of an after-

life, which involve ideas of heaven or hell for 57% gradually wane. By young adulthood only 30% have such perspectives (Schneidman, 1977).

Paradoxically, people in contemporary premodern societies live in the present but are other-worldly oriented, while we living in modern societies generally plan for the future and are this-worldly oriented. Even our religious institutions tend to shift from other-worldly to this-worldly matters, emphasizing the quality of life in the city of man more than a future in the city of God. This aspect of the mortality revolution is attributed by Goldscheider (1976) to the low profile of death in modern society and its segregation within specialized bureaucracies which remove it from the daily affairs of life. No longer is death constantly present, demanding explanation of open, frequent, and conspicuous evidence.

The emergence of secularism, diminishing explanations in terms of "God's will" or "fate," and the alleged decline of religion can hence be traced to declining mortality rates and to the concentration of death among the elderly who already have been removed from the center of family life and the workaday world. "If the revolution in mortality has not directly influenced the shift from religiousness to secularism, it surely has played an integral supporting role" (Goldscheider, 1976, p. 188).

In spite of this secularization of death

> . . . as evidenced by the exalted scientist, the revered doctor, the venerated devices for diagnosis and treatment, and the glorified hospital—the relationship between religion and death is historically rooted and continues, for many, to play an important role in their attitudes (and in their behaviors) toward death (Shneidman, 1976, p. 10).

The central goal of most religions is to foster, stimulate, and sustain the spiritual well-being of their constituents. I shall call attention to three aspects of this topic in reference to death and dying: The avoidance of death is a spiritual phenomenon; the social meanings of death relate to spiritual issues; and the preparation for death is a spiritual task.

Avoidance of Death as a Spiritual Phenomenon

On those rare occasions when people refer to their own death, they typically use the conditional expression, "*If* I die," not the absolute statement implied by saying, "*When* I die." There is a strong tendency to view death as something that happens to other people, not to oneself. As Dumont and Foss (1972) have indicated, Americans collectively and individually simultaneously accept and deny death. On the conscious, intellectual level individual persons recognize that death is inevitable, but on a generally unconscious, emotional plane they tend to hold attitudes of staunch denial. The denial stems from emotionally unacceptable eventualities of separation from loved ones and from worldly pleasures, cessation of the physical self, implicit failure, and the "possibility of eternal damnation" (p. 104).

Contrasting conclusions emerge from viewing death from the perspective of only one side of the ambivalent subject; yet the fear of what may lie beyond the grave may have a great deal to do with personal and societal evasions of death, evasions that have made death a taboo subject, a "pornography" to be avoided in polite society, a phenomenon to hide as if it represents a failure of which to be ashamed. Even during the recent surge of interest in lectures, courses of study, conferences, and books that deal with death and dying, the actual phenomenon remains relatively remote from the daily lives of almost everyone except the people employed in the funeral industry.

Millions of Americans have never seen a corpse. When death does strike in a family, the bereaved, particularly men, are encouraged to hide their grief and disguise their mourning. Most funerals are attended by relatively few friends and relatives of the deceased, and they are conducted in funeral chapels rather than the home or place of worship of the person who died. The embalming arts aim to make the body look younger and more lifelike than it did for years before the death. Typical funeral rites are designed to camouflage the fact of death by reflecting the optimistic framework of contemporary value structures (Berger & Lieban, 1960). Religious people join others in using euphemisms to disguise the fact of death; we cannot refer directly to death, dead people, and corpses, but must instead talk about "passing on," "the late Mr. Smith," and "the deceased." (Of course, some Christian euphemisms like "gone to be with the Lord," "asleep in Christ," "promoted to her eternal reward," and "in glory" have deep theological significance to those who truly appreciate the theological argot.)

Even Elisabeth Kubler-Ross, "the chief evangelist of the gospel of courage in the face of death," in her efforts to teach more effective ways to face death has been accused of speaking "the language of evasion" (Mark, 1979). She is doing "battle with fearsome death by denying its existence" in her portrait of dying people:

> We hear the lie in her promise that a dying man (or woman, or a child) becomes "creative beyond any expectations"; we hear it when she asks us to think of a terminal illness "not as a destructive, negative force, but as one of the windstorms in life that will enhance" our "inner growth"; we hear it in her assurance that death is no more than a "transition to yet another form of existence." And we know it is a lie, finally, when we look at the photographs of Beth's skeletal frame, Louise's weary eyes, Jamie's limp and vulnerable body (Mark, 1979).

Behind much of this denial and avoidance of death lie questions about the meaning of life and the ultimate destiny of humanity. What if the Bible is indeed true in its twofold declaration that all human beings have an appointment to die, and after that comes judgment (Hebrews 9:27)? What if the "confrontation with the ultimate" is in fact an unavoidable "meeting with the sacred for everyone" (Veatch, 1974, p. 9)? And what if there is a spiritual death—"the wages of sin" (Romans 6:23)—that is even more to be feared than physical death? It is deceptively simpler to avoid such existential theological questions by unconscious denial of death than it is to confront them realistically with the aid of the resources of Judeo-Christian revelation and faith.

It has been said, partly in jest, that "the mortality rate is one hundred percent." Life itself can be interpreted as the process of dying, for it is "an incurably fatal disease" (Kelley, 1972, p. ix). We are born to live, but we are also born to die. Possibly everything else in our lives is influenced to some extent by that fact. Dag Hammarskjold (1966) expressed this in one of his "markings":

> No choice is uninfluenced by the way in which the personal-ity regards its destiny, and the body its death. In the last analysis, it is our conception of death which decides our answers to all the questions that life puts to us. That is why it requires its proper place and time—if need be, with right of precedence. Hence, too, the necessity of preparing for it (p. 160).

Similarly, Tournier (1972) pointed out that

> In the last analysis all anxiety is reduced to anxiety about death. Proof of this is the large number of stories in which a man freed from the fear of death is seen to be freed from all other fears; he has no more fear of anything or anyone; no one can overcome him, even by killing him. Nevertheless, the sociologists are right: men do not talk much about this anxiety concerning the threat of death. That is because all men attempt to repress it (p. 216).

Tournier (1972) goes on to indicate that the mystery of death obsesses humankind; yet much conversation is no more than reassuring diversion to avoid the problems of death, and sooth-ing talk often represents "an ineffective attempt to get rid of a latent, blind anxiety" (p. 217). To overcome ageism, we must also overcome the taboo on death. "Who can deny that the meaning of life is death, since it is a journey whose final destination is death?" (p. 218). The meaning of death is a central religious question. The largely unconscious attempt to avoid it is a deeply spiritual phenomenon.

SPIRITUAL ISSUES IN THE SOCIAL MEANINGS OF DEATH

In spite of the denial and avoidance of death in our culture, there is also paradoxically a great deal of exposure to violent death through the mass media with their news of warfare, crime, accidents, victims of drug abuse, and particularly their fictional depictions of violence. When a child is informed that his grandfather died, he may even ask, "Who shot him?" (*Time*, 1965, p. 52).

> Significantly, we as media consumers are more familiar with death by disaster than we are with death by disease. Children who have never attended a funeral or seen a corpse have seen thousands of killings on television. Most of us know more about how to kill another person than about how to treat the dying or comfort the bereaved (Fulton & Markusen, 1979).

The social significance of death, the interpretations we make of it, and the role it plays in our lives are largely shaped by the society and subcultures of which we are a part. We already have noted the denial of death and repression of grief which are so widespread in the United States. The decline of mourning ceremonies has removed much of the opportunity for survivors to experience significant social support during the period of adjustment to a new mode of life. But even before that time, persons who are known to be dying are often bereft of opportunities that could make their closing days, weeks, or months much easier to bear.

"Dying is a social passage" (Kart, Metress, & Metress, 1978, p. 265) in which actions and choices of other people greatly affect what happens to the dying person. The interpretation of the transition depends on the social constructions of reality accepted by death's anticipated victim and by the others who are a part of his or her social milieu. If death ends all except whatever pseudo-immortality is gained through biological offspring, memories in the minds of the bereaved, creative contributions in science, art, or literature, other products of one's work, or the impact of a person upon the history of the times, then the transition is from life to extinction, annihilation, nothingness. If death marks a transition from one form of life to another, as in various versions of reincarnation, that transition represents entering a different life in an endless succession of existences or repeating one's reappearances on a fatalistic treadmill. If death opens the door to a judgment hall where one's good deeds will be weighed against the bad, there may well be fear that scales may tilt in the wrong direction. But if death is interpreted in the Christian sense of being a transition from an imperfect body in an imperfect world to a glorified and eternal state of perfection because of God's gift of salvation, then it may be viewed as a joyful victory (I Corinthians, 15), and one may declare with St. Paul, "For me to live is Christ and to die is gain" (Philippians 1:21). The spiritual outlook makes a tremendous difference to the process of both living and dying.

Each stage in the human life cycle can be seen as preparation for the next. Each has developmental tasks

> ... successful achievement of which leads to [the individual's] happiness and to success with later tasks, while failure leads to unhappiness in the individual, disapproval by the society, and difficulty with later tasks (Havighurst, 1953, p. 2).

Transcending the ordinary in life to endow it with extraordinary significance, quickening the dull, taken-for-granted routines and making them part of the "eternal now," and gaining or retaining meaningfulness while giving up the old and moving with joy and confidence into the new are among the functions of religion in aiding these developmental tasks. Spiritual well-being pertains to reflective transcendence of "the structures of everyday existence" and the ability to "appropriate the meanings, values, and symbolic resources available to them." This transcending process becomes a guiding light through the transition points, including that from old age to death, "the ultimate transition." (Brewer, 1979, p. 109)

One's philosophy of life—and hence of death—is therefore crucial. This philosophy is religious or pseudo-religious, implicitly if not explicitly including spiritual components. Belief or nonbelief in life after death, in heaven and hell, in supernatural rewards and punishments, or in the eternal bliss of those who have faith in Jesus Christ (to mention but a few of these spiritually oriented perspectives) can make a great difference in one's manner of living and dying. The eternal dimension of one's life is constituted by conceptions of the Eternal One, what we think to be the essence of the human-divine relationship, and how we conceive of time and eternity (Abernethy, 1975). Part of the life review that many people make during their later years involves finding "meaning in life's ending in order to give it dignity and to leave a benediction behind us" (Abernethy, p. 156), as well as making sense of the events that have occurred in previous years. The spiritually healthy person

> . . . has a vibrant expectancy, which is what hope means when understood theologically. For it is assured that the perfection of satisfaction that is not yet attained, will come to it at last. There is a principle of life itself in hope for human beings: we are alive to the extent that we live in eager anticipation of the yet-to-be. The presence or absence of this anticipation is what distinguishes, for instance, between one aged person and another: if we say an aged person is still youthful, it is because he or she still looks forward eagerly to the future (Fallding, 1979, p. 34).

Hope, however, does not unrealistically deny the presence of sin and evil in the world. On the contrary, the assumption that there is sin somewhere in the midst of personal and social problems implies that intervention to repair, correct, or meliorate that evil which involves me or others is both a possibility and an obligation.

> Hence sin is the only hopeful view. . . . If the concept of personal responsibility and answerability for ourselves and for others were to return to common acceptance, hope would return to the world with it! (Menninger, 1973, p. 188)

When it has a solid spiritual foundation, "a confident hope concerning the unknown that the patients face . . . is able again and again to give substance to their belief that death is not the end" (Saunders, 1977, p. 175), even for those dying people who reside in a hospice during the closing weeks of their earthly lives.

Preparation for Death as a Spiritual Task

Maggie Kuhn (Hessel, 1977), the famous founder of the Gray Panthers, has said that

> The goal of those who have lived into old age is to be mature, developing, growing adults. Growth is spiritual. Where there is commitment to change and action, there is also some religious motivation, some spiritual growth going on (p. 29).

Such growth, as we indicated earlier, includes preparation for the ultimate transition of the life cycle, death.

It is most unfortunate that many expect the elderly and the dying merely to sit back and passively wait for the inevitable. It is far more consistent with the realities of human experience, as well as with the theologies of Christianity and Judaism, to declare that the art of successful dying is the art of living the abundant life of service to God and fellow men. Elsewhere I have shown that the elderly person who is a Christian need never be "laid on the shelf," as long as he or she retains consciousness and is not in such extreme suffering that all thoughts except those of pain are squeezed from the mind. Even after declining health and strength make it impossible to perform volunteer services and deeds of kindness to others, such persons can still be active in service to God, the church, and people through prayers on their behalf (Gray & Moberg, 1977, p. 178).

The process of giving, following the example of God who is the perfect Giver, can continue even after death if arrangements have been made in advance to donate the body or its parts for transplants of skin, corneas, kidneys, or other organs, or for medical training and research. Impending death need not end our giving to others if appropriate legal and other arrangements are made before the final departure from this life.

Spiritual preparation for death includes more than serving others. Settling old accounts with God and man through confessing and atoning for sins and mistakes of the past is often necessary and rewarding. Reminiscing that helps to integrate the personality can be very fruitful, most of all when explicit attention is given to the spiritual component of one's life. Taking care of material and economic affairs pertaining to one's will, estate, medical expenses, and funeral is clearly a spiritual task when viewing the person wholistically, and most expressly when considering the Judeo-Christian concept that people are but temporary stewards of what God has entrusted to them.

Facilitating good psychological and emotional adjustments for oneself and others and approaching the closing years and days of life as a developmental task instead of in submission to blind fate are constructive uses of one's time and energy. Renewal and fulfillment can be experienced in the later years through religious faith, participation and experience in a community of faith, and ministries with and for other older persons, as well as through second careers (McClellan, 1977).

Loneliness can be dispelled and widowed persons can find a family surrogate in religious organizations (Kivett, 1979). Comforting others can provide outlets for such service, for many elderly persons face an overload of bereavement and do not complete the grief process before another friend or loved one dies. Taking leave of one friend after another, the elderly person must eventually mourn his or her own impending departure (Abernethy, 1975). Widow-to-widow services, as well as less formalized activities to relate to the grief of others, are helpful to all who are involved; the providers of services are also recipients. Spiritual symbols, familiar comforting words of scripture, and rituals reminding of God's love and presence are tremendously helpful when facing the sorrows and trials of life.

> The two greatest biblical symbols—the Suffering Servant and the Cross—teach us that it is not just I, nor even all humankind, but that God himself is a God who is acquainted with grief and knows its sorrows. (Abernethy, 1975, pp. 140–141)

The unconscious fear of death in our society makes many members of the helping professions avoid the dying and even the elderly. Their thanatophobia contributes to gerontophobia, the prejudicial attitudes that lie behind the discriminatory practices of ageism. This, in turn, creates efforts to prolong life just as long as possible, even for elderly persons suffering from incurable conditions. In effect, such efforts merely postpone death and prolong the dying process. Death is equated with failure—failure of the medical profession, of the dying person, of his or her family, and of anyone else who has been in close association with the one who is dying. If there were a more realistic orientation, people would be more likely to experience their right to die in dignity.

Spiritual orientations can help to alleviate these fears and injustices in our society (Moberg, 1971). Their presence or absence and the shape they take help to determine whether people speak of "the tragedy of death" or "the release of death"—release from bondage to the limitations of this life into the glorious freedom of the children of God; release from suffering, illness, and pain into the joys of fully experiencing God's kingdom; release from the limitations of material, social, or psychological poverty into the wealth of the heavenly Father; release from anxieties and fears into the experience of unthreatened security; release from the demands and pressures of temporal life into the rest and peace of eternal life.

Anticipation of the end of one's life may lead to reorganization of one's use of time priorities. All possessions and experiences become transient. Feelings of meaninglessness may develop, for if anything were attempted, it might be either short-lived or unfinished. When people were asked what they would do if they were to die in 30 days, the elderly were less likely than younger persons to change at all. But when asked what they would change if they had only six months until death, nearly three times as many older persons reported they would "spend their remaining time in prayer, reading, contemplation, or other activities that reflected inner life, spiritual needs, or withdrawal" (Kart et al., 1978, p. 252).

When death actually approaches and physicians become aware of it, they often are reluctant to inform the patients of impending death for fear that the social and psychological problems of dying will be more acute if the patient knows the prognosis; they also feel that loss of hope will hasten death and prevent the remotely possible cure. A large majority of people who have been surveyed, however, prefer to know the truth so that they will have the opportunity to settle material affairs, family business, matters of conscience, and relationships with God.

The "big lie" can be told by accurate medical statements filled with so much technical language that the patient does not understand that the diagnosis is one of a fatal illness. The doctor may then pretend to have told the patient the truth when in fact there was no effective communication at all. This, and refusing to tell, can have a negative reaction in more than the immediate sense, for the family and others will recognize that truth is not always told in the physician-patient relationship. They then may begin to fear that they cannot depend on whatever good news they may receive in the future, and a "demonic, anxiety-provoking breakdown of trust," which is essential for good medical care, may result (Veatch, 1974; Kart et al., 1978).

"The spiritual need for a man to know that he is dying may well take precedence over material matters in the terminal phase" (Hinton, 1976, p. 304). This knowledge gives a person the opportunity to turn or return to religious faith in preparation for eternal life.

> A conspiracy of silence and deceit around the patient is a dehumanizing way to live—and to die. The goal should be to humanize the process of dying. That does not involve "managing" the patient, a misguided approach which has a demeaning, dehumanizing connotation. The dying patient must not be managed but cared for. (Veatch, 1974, p. 34)

A similar lack of support that hastens deterioration and tends to intensify the patient's fears occurs when family members refuse to admit that their loved one is not likely to recover. When no one will talk with a person about the likelihood of approaching death, he or she loses the opportunity to express emotions freely and to do the "death work" that can help the person take leave of this life with equanimity and peace.

Good communication, both verbal and nonverbal, is an important responsibility of all who attend to the dying person. Nurses who are sensitive to spiritual needs can give patients a sense of security and comfort in their frightening condition and strange environment. The philosophy of caring for the whole person includes responsibility for spiritual needs (Fish & Shelly, 1978). The church and its groups and members similarly can serve spiritual needs while bridging the total span of life as no other institution can (Mason, 1978).

Every ill and dying person has the basic human right to receive spiritual care (Lichtenberger, 1979). Yet even the alleged "spiritual care" that is given can be provided so perfunctorily (Sudnow, 1967) that it is almost meaningless, or under such conditions that patients are frightened because they were given sacraments which they interpret as implying that they are about to die (Strauss, 1975). Such mistiming in the services of a chaplain or priest is more likely in institutional settings than in a home (Strauss, 1975).

The fear of death is more often alleviated than increased by religious influences. Leming (1975) found only three studies in the social psychology literature in which religiosity was correlated with death fear, but 10 in which religious factors were significantly related to the reduction of fears and anxieties concerning death (Gray & Moberg, 1977 pp. 137–138). Since fear of the unknown is one part of the trauma that is often associated with the dying process, a formal system of religious beliefs assimilated by the person makes easier the transition "into that life for which we are made" (Veatch, 1974, p. 7).

Abernethy (1975, pp. 134–135) tells the story of a Vermont pastor who went with heavy heart to pray for elderly Asa, who had been feverishly ill for weeks. He came away lighter in heart and spirit because of Asa's response: "I don't mind goin', not a mite, but I do hate t' go in this dilapidated condition." We may fail to learn about many persons who "don't mind goin' " just because we are too reluctant to speak naturally and openly about the impending experience.

CONCLUSION

Numerous hypotheses were suggested in the above remarks, even though they were not presented in a formal scientific manner. There is a need for research on almost every aspect of the process of death and dying, particularly on the significance of spiritual factors in the process. This requires an appropriate merger of skills and perspectives from theology with those of the social and behavioral sciences (see Becker, 1977). It demands the construction of instruments for the measurement of spiritual well-being and other concepts required for effective research (see Chapter 1 of Moberg, 1979). It necessitates recognition of the wholistic nature of people, all of whom are spiritual as well as physical and mental creatures.

Unfortunately, discussion of spiritual well-being can be diverted quickly into subsidiary topics like mysticism, conversion, and mental health, then left without any direct attention itself (Fallding, 1979). This, however, is no excuse for giving up before we even begin the effort.

> Old age and death thrust themselves upon us with inevitability. But we can positively accept and affirm that which in a real sense is thrust upon us. That acceptance holds for life itself. Not one of us chose to be born. Life was thrust upon us, yet we do have the option of accepting and affirming the life we did not choose. . . . So it is with old age and death. Paradoxically, aging and death thrust themselves upon us, but we can positively accept and affirm both. (Stagg, 1978, p. 15)

Dag Hammarskjold (1966), shares many of his own spiritual reflections in *Markings,* expressing a similar positive outlook toward death: "Do not seek Death. Death will find you. But seek the road which makes death a fulfillment" (p. 159).

Those who recognize that the essence of humanity resides in the human soul can face death optimistically, seeing it as a transition of the immortal spirit, a fulfillment of the pilgrimage of life on earth. Such persons "rejoice in the hope of the glory of God" (Romans, 5:2), for they know that

> The body that is sown is perishable, [but] it is raised imperishable; it is sown in dishonor, it is raised in glory; it is sown in weakness, it is raised in power; it is sown a natural

body, it is raised a spiritual body (I Corinthians, 15:42–44, New International Version).

Their spiritual well-being is grounded in a faith that sustains them through all of the experiences of life, including dying. Nurtured by the rich legacy of centuries of religious experience, their definition of the meaning and nature of death as a transitional stage of human existence provides the foundation for facing the termination of their own earthly life with equanimity and hope.

REFERENCES

Abernethy, J. B. *Old is not a four-letter word.* Nashville: Abingdon Press, 1975.

Becker, E. The heroics of everyday life: A theorist of death confronts his own end. In S. H. Zarit (Ed.), *Readings in aging and death.* New York: Harper & Row, 1977.

Berger, P. & Lieban, R. Cultural value structure and funeral practices in the United States. *Koelner Zeitschrift fuer Soziologie und Sozialpsychologie,* 1960, *12,* 224–236.

Brewer, E. D. C. Life stages and spiritual well-being. In D. O. Moberg (Ed.), *Spiritual well-being: Sociological perspectives.* Washington, D.C.: University Press of America, 1979.

Dumont, R. G., & Foss, D. C. *The American view of death: Acceptance or denial?* Cambridge, Massachusetts: Schenkman Publishing Company, 1972.

Fallding, H. Spiritual well-being as a variety of good morale. In D. O. Moberg (Ed.), *Spiritual well-being: Sociological perspectives.* Washington, D.C.: University Press of America, 1979.

Fish, S. & Shelly, J. A. *Spiritual care: The nurse's role.* Downers Grove, Illinois: InterVarsity Press, 1978.

Fulton, R., Markusen, E. Dying with gusto: Popular culture offers feast of violence and death. Milwaukee Journal (February 4, Accent Section), 1979, p. 11.

Goldscheider, C. The mortality revolution. In E. S. Shneidman (Ed.), *Death: Current perspectives.* Palo Alto, California: Mayfield Publishing Company, 1976.

Gray, R. M. & Moberg, D. O. *The church and the older person* (rev. ed.). Grand Rapids, Michigan: Wm. B. Eerdmans Publishing, 1977.

Hammarskjold, D. *Markings.* (L. Sjöberg & W. H. Auden, trans.). New York: Alfred A. Knopf, 1966.

Havighurst, R. J. *Human development and education.* New York: Longmans, 1953.

Hessel, D. (Ed.). *Maggie Kuhn on aging: A dialogue.* Philadelphia: Westminster Press, 1977.

Hinton, J. Speaking of death with the dying. In E. S. Shneidman (Ed.), *Death: Current perspectives.* Palo Alto, California: Mayfield Publishing Company, 1976.

Kart, C. S., Metress, E. S., & Metress, J. F. *Aging and health.* Menlo Park, California: Addison-Wesley Publishing, 1978.

Kelley, M. *Why conservative churches are growing.* New York: Harper & Row, 1972.

Kivett, V. R. Discriminators of loneliness among the rural elderly: Implications for intervention. *The Gerontologist,* 1979, *19,* 108–115.

Leming, M. R. *The relationship between religiosity and the fear of death.* Unpublished Ph.D. dissertation in sociology, University of Utah, 1975.

Levinson, D. J. *The seasons of a man's life.* New York: Alfred A. Knopf, 1978.

Lichtenberger, R. E. The patient's right to spiritual care. *The Nurses Lamp: Bulletin of Nurses Christian Fellowship,* 1979, *30,* (4, March), 2–3.

Mark, R. The gospel of courage: An evasion? (review of *To live until we say goodbye* by Elisabeth Kubler-Ross). *Wall Street Journal,* January 3, 1979, p. 8.

Mason, J. M. *The fourth generation.* Minneapolis: Augsburg Publishing House, 1978.

McClellan, R. W. *Claiming a frontier: Ministry and older people.* Los Angeles: University of Southern California Press, 1977.

Menninger, K. *Whatever became of sin?* New York: Hawthorn Books, 1973.

Moberg, D. O. *Spiritual well-being: Background and issues.* Washington, D.C.: White House Conference on Aging, 1971.

Moberg, D. O. (Ed.) *Spiritual well-being: Sociological perspectives.* Washington, D.C.: University Press of America, 1979.

Saunders, C. Dying they live: St. Christopher's Hospice. In H. Feifel

(Ed.), *New meanings of death*. New York: McGraw-Hill Book Company, 1977.

Schneidman, E. S. (Ed.). *Death: Current perspectives,* Palo Alto, California: Mayfield Publishing Company, 1976.

Schneidman, E. S. The college student and death. In H. Feifel (Ed.), *New Meanings of Death*. New York: McGraw-Hill Book Company, 1977.

Stagg, F. *Biblical perspectives on aging*. Athens, Georgia: National Interfaith Coalition on Aging, 1978.

Strauss, A. L. *Chronic illness and the quality of life*. St. Louis, Missouri: C. V. Mosby Company, 1975.

Sudnow, D. *Passing on: The social organization of dying*. Englewood Cliffs, New Jersey: Prentice-Hall, 1967.

Time Essay. On death as a constant companion. *Time*, 1965, *86* (20, Nov. 12), 52–53.

Tournier, P. *Learn to grow old* (E. Hudson, trans.). New York: Harper & Row, 1972.

Veatch, R. *Death and dying*. Chicago: Claretian Publications, 1974.

Acknowledgments

Chapters in this volume are based on presentations selected from the Fifth Annual Gerontology Institute held at Sangamon State University.

The Gerontology Institute is an annual cooperative effort developed by the Sangamon State University Gerontology Task Force whose membership includes agencies and organizations in the State of Illinois with interests in gerontology and geriatrics. The Task Force is chaired by the Director of the Illinois Department on Aging.

Co-sponsors of the Gerontology Institute 1979 included the Illinois Department on Aging, the Illinois Office of Education, and the Illinois Funeral Directors Association.

INDEX